Aspects of
POLITICAL
DEVELOPMENT

The Little, Brown Series

in Comparative Politics

Under the Editorship of

GABRIEL A. ALMOND

JAMES S. COLEMAN

LUCIAN W. PYE

AN ANALYTIC STUDY

Aspects of
POLITICAL
DEVELOPMENT

Lucian W. Pye
Massachusetts Institute of Technology

Boston and Toronto

LITTLE, BROWN AND COMPANY

Published simultaneously in Canada
by Little, Brown & Company (Canada) Limited

PRINTED IN THE UNITED STATES OF AMERICA

Foreword

THE Little, Brown Series in Comparative Politics has three main objectives. First, it will meet the need of teachers to deal with both western and non-western countries in their introductory course offerings. Second, by following a common approach in the analysis of individual political systems, it will make it possible for teachers to compare these countries systematically and cumulatively. And third, it will contribute toward reestablishing the classic relationship between comparative politics and political theory, a relationship which has been neglected in recent decades. In brief, the series seeks to be global in scope, genuinely introductory and comparative in character, and concerned with broadening and deepening our understanding of the nature and variety of political systems.

The series has two parts: the Country Studies and the Analytic Studies. The Country Studies deal with a set of problems and processes deriving from a functional, as against a purely structural, approach to the study of political systems. We are gratified that the participants, all of them mature scholars with original insights of their own, were willing to organize their discussions around a common set of functional topics in the interest of furthering comparisons. At the same time, each author has been urged to adapt the common framework to the special problems of the country he is discussing and to express his own theoretical point of view.

An introductory book, *The Study of Comparative Politics,* written by Gabriel A. Almond and G. Bingham Powell, provides an analytical supplement to the Country Studies. It also opens our set of Analytic Studies, which will offer basic discussions of such topics as political change in the emerging nations, comparative analyses of interest groups, political socialization, political communication, political culture, and the like. We hope these books will prove to be useful and stimulating supplements to the Country Series as well as points of departure in more advanced courses.

In *Aspects of Political Development* Lucian W. Pye has drawn together some of his recent writings on the problems of the developing countries and added considerable original material to present a coherent book on a topic of broad public interest. In Part I, he deals with general problems in understanding the development process, while Part II reviews more specific policy problems. The focus of the entire work is upon the prospects of democratic and human development in the transitional societies.

A subsequent volume of the Analytic Studies is planned which will deal systematically with the larger problem of political change.

Gabriel A. Almond
James S. Coleman
Lucian W. Pye

Preface

THE EMERGENCE of the new states of Africa and Asia has
challenged the perspectives and the theoretical capacities
of all the social science disciplines. Academic fields whose
universe was once comfortably limited to Western societies and
maybe a few primitive cultures have suddenly been called upon
to yield knowledge about the profound but erratic forms of
change that are sweeping much of the world. In discipline after
discipline, research and teaching is in the process of responding to the need for greater understanding about all aspects of
change in what is recognized as a new category of social systems, that of the transitional societies.

Initially the burden of providing intellectual guidance for
the developmental process in the new states seemed naturally
to fall to economics. The people in the emerging countries
seem to attach the highest priorities to economic development,
and within economics there was a traditional concern about
both the explanation of economic growth and the practice of
advising policy-makers. More recently, however, anxiety over
the prospects of the new states has shifted increasingly to the
political sphere, and political science is confronted with a se-
vere test: Can the oldest of the social sciences provide understanding and guidance about the great revolution of our era?

The awkward truth is that political science has been somewhat embarrassed by the concept of political development
which is novel to the discipline's lexicon. Classical political
theory recognized different forms of political systems, but it

vii

had little to say about the theory of nation-building or the phenomenon of political development as it is now conceived in the new states. But the urgent need for new concepts and empirical research is being met, and the result is a new subject for political science. The established fields of comparative politics and political theory have generally recognized the importance of this new subject of political development.

The purpose of this book is to introduce students to an exciting and growing field of study. The student should be properly warned that the field has many rough edges, little central coherence, but a vigorously expanding literature and great opportunities for research and intellectual creativity. Students who do become interested in the fundamental problems of the emerging states can expect to move to the frontiers of a discipline in a very short period of time and to contribute substantially to a great public policy problem of our time and to a significant advance in human knowledge.

In this volume are brought together, in revised form, various journal articles and chapters of symposia I have written over the last few years which deal with both the social scientists' problem of conceptualizing and theorizing about the processes of political development and the problems of policy-makers in the underdeveloped areas. This work does not attempt to formulate a general theory about political development; rather, it contains numerous ideas and concepts I feel will be of value in eventually building more systematic theories . . . nor is this book an inclusive review of all the public-policy problems inherent in the condition of the new states. The focus, instead, is upon some of the more critical issues.

Much of the material making up this book was originally written during the course of my research at the Center for International Studies at the Massachusetts Institute of Technology. That research was supported by a grant from the Carnegie Corporation, and I am happy to express my appreciation to that foundation for its assistance.

I am greatly indebted to Richard W. Hatch of the M.I.T. Center for International Studies for thoughtfully reviewing the material and advising that much of it could be organized into a coherent work. Above all, his remarkable understanding of what comprises a book has made this volume possible. At all stages Alice Preston magically transformed my illegible script into typed manuscript.

Also, I must acknowledge the gracious permission given by several publishers to reproduce excerpts of material originally appearing in their publications. Chapter I incorporates sections of "The Political Context of National Development," from *Development Administration: Concepts and Problems,* edited by Irving Swerdlow and published by Syracuse University Press in 1963. Chapter II follows "The Concept of Political Development," in *The Annals of the American Academy of Social and Political Science,* Spring 1965. Chapter IV is based in part upon "Democracy, Modernization, and Nation Building," in *Self-government in Modernizing Nations,* edited by J. Roland Pennock and published in 1964 by Prentice-Hall. Chapter VI is essentially "Law and the Dilemma of Stability and Change in the Modernization Process," *Vanderbilt Law Review,* Vol. 17, No. 1 (December 1963). Chapter VII is a revision of "The Roots of Insurgency and the Commencement of Rebellions," from *Internal War,* edited by Harry Eckstein, Free Press, 1964. Chapter VIII is based on pages from *Communications and Political Development,* published in 1963 by Princeton University Press. Chapter IX is a modification of "Armies in the Process of Political Modernization," in *The Role of the Military in Developing Countries,* edited by John J. Johnson and published by the Princeton University Press, 1962. I have also inserted a few pages from *Politics, Personality, and Nation Building,* Yale University Press, 1962. All rights on the reproduced materials are, of course, still reserved by the original publishers.

Cambridge, Mass.   Lucian W. Pye
August 1965

TO LYNDY,

CHRIS,

AND VIRGINIA

Table of Contents

Aspects of
POLITICAL
DEVELOPMENT

PART I

The General Issues
of Political Development

CHAPTER I

Political Development in
Historical Perspective

WORLD WAR I ended on the theme of "national self-determination," and the world was dazzled by the array of new nations to emerge in Eastern Europe and out of the breakup of the Hapsburg and Turkish empires. But the world soon learned to recognize the pretensions of new states and to accept the paradox that communities conceived as independent through the vigorous assertion of the universality of the democratic ethic were likely to slip into autocratic ways. World War II ended with the breaking up of far greater empires, and the world has suddenly discovered it has more "new states" than old ones. Again the theme of democracy and liberal aspirations accompanied the birth of nations, and again performances are falling far below expectations.

Political development has proved to be a difficult, albeit exciting, process. The imagination of a whole generation has been captured by the prospect of impoverished and tradition-bound peoples finding a new place in the sun. At a time when the great powers have become superpowers and the gap between the "haves" and the "have nots" has never been greater the focus of world politics has been dramatically concentrated on the efforts of the weak and the aspiring. Although World War II presumably taught the world the importance of respon-

3

sible power in preserving order, and the revolution of technology has provided unimagined new levels of power, the day-to-day process of international events has elevated to critical status developments in still inchoate nations.

The very vocabulary of world politics has been engulfed by terms and programs related to a new view of nation-building — the developing areas, the emerging nations, Afro-Asian states, economic development plans, charismatic leaders, technical assistance, Point Four, the Third World, neutralism, the revolution of rising expectations, foreign aid, the Alliance for Progress, Peace Corps, modernization, intellectual elites and peasant masses, one-party rule, foreign technicians, international lending agencies, and so on and so forth. The strong and rich governments have initiated novel programs to facilitate the domestic development of the weak and poor, and the new professions of the technical advisers and development administrators have come into being. The problem of the American serving abroad is no longer that of representing American power but of learning how to be effective in helping others to achieve their ambitions of development.[1]

It might seem an anachronism that at the very time when advances in science have brought us to the threshold of space exploration and the automation of industry, so much attention must be given to advancing in pitifully modest ways the agricultural technologies of peasant villagers or in training people to elementary industrial skills. But there is a definite link between the most advanced miracles of twentieth-century technology and the efforts to speed the breakdown in age-old traditional habits of life. For it is the scientific revolution which has given man the vision that he can, according to his will, change the circumstances of his life and purposefully create new environments for his societies.[2]

[1] For an excellent analysis of the meaning of overseas service for individual Americans see: Harlan Cleveland, Gerard J. Mangone, and John Clarke Adams, *The Overseas Americans* (New York: McGraw-Hill, 1960).

[2] For a provocative discussion of the relationship of science and technology to development see David E. Apter's contribution to *Discussion at Bellagio*, K. H. Silvert, ed. (New York: American Universities Field Staff, 1964).

Historically it was unquestionably accepted that man's political and social orders were largely preordained by the particular histories of each community. Men might dream of Utopia and leaders might inspire incremental improvements, but the weight of reality suggested that at best there could only be gradual advancement. Indeed the burden of relatively recent "scientific" sociology held that man was probably the prisoner of impersonal ecological laws that governed his condition and did not include much room for voluntarism and conscious efforts at manipulating change. Revolutions might occur, but the wise man knew that little changed and progress was slow. With explosive suddenness this generation came to a new view of man's potency for directing change. Overnight, leaders and would-be leaders believed that new conditions of social, economic, and political life could be readily created out of purposeful planning. Nations which once took generations to mold could now hopefully be established in short order, and with purposeful political development all other forms of development might instantly follow.

There was much nobility in this new vision of man's potentialities. There was also much innocence. For the last decade has seen an endless record of bold experiments becoming deep sources of frustration. In many quarters the easy optimism of the first years of the era of nation-building has given way to cynicism and feelings of futility. It has become evident that just as Rome was not built in a day, the new orders in Asia and Africa cannot be established overnight.

Irrespective of expectations, the problems of nation-building and political development remain. Somehow the peoples of Asia and Africa must find new arrangements that will give them satisfaction and dignity. Therefore if we have the courage to avoid the easy extremes of innocent optimism and futile cynicism, we are left with the pressing challenge of learning more about the nature of political development and the limits for effectively accelerating purposeful change. To begin this search for understanding it is appropriate to find a historical perspective on how the concept of the nation-state was gradually diffused outward from Europe to eventually encompass the entire world. For the essence of contemporary political development is the realization of that extraordinarily complex human institution, the modern nation-state, which in turn was originally produced within the European state system.[3]

THE DIFFUSION OF THE CONCEPT OF THE STATE

Fundamental among the many themes running through the exceedingly complex story of the diffusion of Western civilization throughout the world and the establishment of the era of Western colonialism would be the persisting demand by Europeans that human relations, and more particularly the management of disputes, should fall under explicit and universally-based laws. As Europeans moved restlessly into the non-Western world — as traders and merchants, missionaries and adventurers — they carried with them the conviction that all societies should properly be organized as states possessing attributes of sovereignty and adhering to rules of law. Wherever the European went, one of his first revealing queries was, "Who is in charge here?" According to the logic of the European mind every territory should fall under some sovereignty and all people in the same geographic locations should have a common loyalty and the same legal obligations. Also, in the early clashes of culture the European response was to search for legal redress, and the absence of a recognizable legal order must have made life uncomfortable for these early European adventurers.[4]

For the past three hundred years a constant theme recurring throughout the apparently haphazard process of Western contacts with the rest of the world has been the stubborn and

[3] For a classic statement of the theory of the Western nation-state see Alfred Cobban, *National Self-Determination* (Chicago: University of Chicago Press, 1944); for a contemporary statement see K. H. Silvert, *Expectant Peoples: Nationalism and Development* (New York: Random House, 1964).

[4] The compelling force of legal notions is well documented in the story of the early British attempts to establish diplomatic and commercial relations with Imperial China. It is the central theme in H. B. Morse's three-volume study, *The International Relations of the Chinese Empire* (London: Longmans, Green & Co., 1910).

ceaseless efforts of the European state system to transform all societies into replicas of the nation-state. To the European mind it was inconceivable that anyone might not be governed by an impersonal state and not feel a part of a nation. The European system required all territory to fall under some specific jurisdiction, every person to belong to some polity, and all polities to behave as proper states within the family of nations.

Wherever Europeans have gone they have generally displayed their impatience with any other arrangement of social life and devoted their surplus of energy and resources to the end of bringing others in line with the standards of the modern nation-state. Throughout this period men who felt a responsibility for maintaining the stability and the easy working of the nation-state system regarded as a fundamental threat all domestic forms of authority which failed to meet minimum standards of nation-statehood. This concern has left its mark on the European mind. It is reflected in the intolerance of Westerners toward all who fail to meet these minimum standards — a feeling which is at the same time disturbing to Westerners, acutely conscious as they are of the evils of ethnocentrism.[5] It is also reflected in the Western insistence that societies which do not voluntarily act as nation-states must be compelled to do so even if this means direct assistance and open intervention in their affairs.

This is one way of looking at the long history of Western dealings with the rest of the world. From such a view there is a thread of continuity from the first early efforts of the British and Dutch, the French and the Americans, to persuade the traditional rulers of India and China, of Java and the rest of Asia to adhere to Western notions of international law and usage. When the indirect approach proved inadequate, there came the phase of colonialism during which representatives of the nation-state system imposed upon recalcitrant traditional

5 The ambivalent feelings of British officials in India are well documented in Philip Woodruff, *The Men Who Ruled India* (2 vols., New York: St. Martin's Press, 1954).

societies the infra-structure of the nation-state in the form of Westernized administrative structures. And now that colonialism is ended, we see the United States and others through various forms of foreign aid and technical assistance continuing the effort to shape numerous loosely-structured societies into reasonable facsimiles of the modern nation-state.

It is now evident that we are engaged in a long historical process involving two, not always harmonious, levels of change. The first level of change we can call modernization. This is the process of profound social change in which tradition-bound villages or tribal-based societies are compelled to react to the pressures and demands of the modern, industrialized, and urban-centered world. This process might also be called Westernization, or simply advancement and progress; it might, however, be more accurately termed the diffusion of a world culture — a world culture based on advanced technology and the spirit of science, on a rational view of life, a secular approach to social relations, a feeling for justice in public affairs, and, above all else, on the acceptance in the political realm of the belief that the prime unit of the polity should be the nation-state.

At another level is the historical development of a system of international relations in which the nation-state is again the prime unit. The development and maintenance of the nation-state system has been instrumental in diffusing the elements of modernization throughout the world; and in turn the modernizing process, by creating tensions and instabilities in formerly static societies, has created disruptive forces which threaten the stability of the entire international system of nation-states.

Thus those who feel a sense of responsibility for maintaining international stability are striving to facilitate the process of modernization so that all societies can become stable states while at the same time seeking to prevent this very process of social change from disrupting the stability of the international system. The resulting struggle explains the prime purposes of American foreign-policy efforts in this era.

THE WORLD CULTURE AND PRESSURES FOR
NATION-BUILDING

When the European world first pressed outward and learned of the worlds of Africa and Asia there was some basis of mutuality in the contacts. It would have been hard at the time of these first contacts to predict how the interchange of cultural contacts would affect each side. But at an ever-accelerating rate the direction and the volume of cross-cultural influences has become nearly a uniform pattern of the Western industrial world imposing its practices, standards, techniques, and values upon the non-Western world.

This massive flow of cultural diffusion is most clearly manifest in the political realm. The development of the nation-state is only in part an autonomous, domestic process, for all states are shaped in very fundamental ways by the fact that they are units of a nation-state system, and they are constantly called upon to interact with that system. Indeed, the nation-state has little meaning in isolation, and most of the concepts basic to the operations and organization of the modern nation-state are derived from the standards common to the international community of states. Starting from the problems of defense and foreign policy and carrying over into the fields of membership in the United Nations and the control of international trade and commerce and on into the realm of the domestic management of affairs, a host of very explicit pressures move governments in certain very definite directions.

Although the particular institutional forms of government, the organization of the polity, and the spirit of the political culture all may vary within wide limits, there are certain minimum qualifications of statehood in the international community which place demands upon the development of all nation-states. These demands go beyond just those related to the functional needs of the nation-state system as a whole and reflect what we might call the cultural climate of that system. That is to say, there is also what we may call a "world" or a "cosmopolitan" culture that is closely related to the nation-state system.

We cannot dwell here on the content of the world culture; it is sufficient to observe that it does have a degree of inner coherence, and it is generally recognized as being the essence of modern life. It is based upon a secular rather than a sacred view of human relations, a rational outlook, an acceptance of the substance and spirit of the scientific approach, a vigorous application of an expanding technology, an industrialized organization of production, and a generally humanistic and popularistic set of values for political life.

Once we recognize the demands and the attractions of both the nation-state system and the world culture we can begin to appreciate the basic stresses that must underlie the nation-building process in the new states. We can see that there is a minimum level of what were once Western but are now world standards which the new states must accept if they are to survive in a world of independent nation-states. Thus the international political and cultural fashions of the day set the general direction of development for the new states.

A further complication is that since the diffusion of the world culture can weaken and destroy the structure of traditional societies but cannot so easily reconstitute a more modernized society, the consequence of the international impact has more often been chaos and tension than a new order. It seems that the destruction of old relationships is proceeding at an increasingly faster rate than the pace of social reconstruction, and thus another widening gap seems to exist between the emerging nation-states and the modern nation-states with industrialized economies.

When the European powers first reached out to intervene in the lives of traditional societies and to set in motion the process of change, they invariably relied upon the persisting grip of the ancient, indigenous traditions to maintain the basic fabric of the society. Colonial rule brought radical changes in the formal organization of government, and it set loose swelling waves of change; but colonial rule was possible only as long as the traditional order was able to give structure and form to the society. The handful of Europeans who governed most of Asia and Africa could do their job because the peoples they ruled were still governed throughout the cycle of their lives by traditional systems. Habit, custom, and village relationships gave discipline and order to the lives of most of the people, and the colonial rulers had to treat only with elite relationships at the top of the societies.

However, as the Western impact continued to weaken the old order, the inescapable consequence was a rise in the need for the formal, legal system of government and administration to provide the basis of social order. The eroding of the one system placed greater demands upon the other, and soon it became only a matter of time before the costs of trying to give political order and shape to the disarrayed transitional societies became prohibitive for the colonial powers. Thus, the transfer of sovereignty has often meant a transfer of the costs of and the responsibilities for rebuilding an effective social system.

By weakening the cohesion of societies while simultaneously suggesting the unlimited potentialities of coherent political systems, the diffusion of the world culture has created the cruel but fundamental problem of the underdeveloped areas of today. On the one hand the idea has been spread throughout the world that all people should belong to a nation-state, that the nation-state is the most appropriate and natural unit of political life and should provide the basis for a sense of collective identity. On the other hand the very process that has communicated this idea has also threatened the capacities of people to act effectively in all phases of their political and social life. The acculturation process calls for the creation of all the numerous forms of organization necessary to support the social, political, and economic activities associated with modern life; but at the same time the experience of acculturation taxes the abilities of people to create and maintain modern organizations.[6]

6 For a more extensive discussion of the problems of the diffusion of the world culture in nation-building see Lucian W. Pye, *Politics, Personality, and Nation Building* (New Haven: Yale University Press, 1962) chapter I.

THREE LEVELS OF ORDER

The problem of creating nation-states in societies that were only recently colonial entities or traditional political or even tribal communities is part of a much larger process of building a new world order to replace the international system of the colonial era. The concept that the world community should be organized on the basis of separate, sovereign nation-states had its first impetus out of the settlement of the First World War and the establishment of the League of Nations, and it was further intensified by the creation of the United Nations after World War II. The intensification of the cold war and the helter-skelter pace of formal admission into the United Nations of still incoherent societies as legally sovereign states in recent years has drawn attention away from the fundamental fact that a stable basis for a new world order has yet to be established. As long as it is uncertain what this new order is going to be, there remains considerable confusion about what should be the essential qualities of the nation-state in the contemporary world.[7]

The classical nation-state system which emerged out of the European cultural complex had many distinctive qualities that can no longer be realized. In that system all the member states shared a relatively homogeneous cultural base, particularly as related to the scope and function of government. They shared also a relatively common level of technology; so while one might be "larger" or more "powerful" than another, the question of whether one was "superior" and the other "inferior" was neither appropriate nor frequently raised. Also in the classical system the constituent states represented governments based on distinct institutions which, to a degree, were autonomous of the other spheres of society. This meant that governments could be expected to maintain themselves according to the norms of the international system and not be so vulnerable

[7] For an extensive discussion of the meaning of contemporary "nationalism" and "sovereignty" see Rupert Emerson, *From Empire to Nation* (Cambridge: Harvard University Press, 1959).

to domestic events as to be unable to meet the international standards.[8]

Above all, however, the classical nation-state system was premised upon certain assumptions about the nature of a "state" and about the characteristics of "sovereignty." Specifically, it was assumed that the ultimate test of sovereignty was the ability of a government to commit the society over which it claimed to rule to courses of action of indefinitely long-time duration. To have sovereignty was to be able to make treaties and to insure that they were carried out. The concept of sovereignty in classical international law was thus directly related to the concept of effective action.

In the present day setting it is clear that sovereignty no longer is tied to the capacity for effective action. Sovereignty is seen more often as a universal right. But the question remains: what kind of world order is possible where there are such great differences in the culture forms and technological levels of the various entities claiming sovereignty? As long as there is confusion about essential forms of any evolving world order, there will be confusion about what are the appropriate standards of performance for an aspiring nation-state.

The problem is more complicated, however, for just as there is confusion at the highest level of the international order so is there confusion at the lowest level of the political system, and this is at the level of the individual and what it means to be a citizen in modern times. In all the transitional societies people are going through a profound process of psychological adjustment as their old social order is disrupted and the relationships of family, tribe, clan, and village are upset and new patterns of relationships are emerging. These psychological disruptions can create deep feelings of ambivalence and uncertainty that can inhibit all effective action and stimulate widespread feelings of anxiety and alienation.[9]

[8] The classic nation-state system is well described in Hans Morgenthau, *Politics Among Nations* (3rd edn., New York: Alfred A. Knopf, 1960).

[9] For excellent introductions to these psychological problems of adjustment to change see Leonard W. Doob, *Becoming More Civilized: A Psy-*

This basic uncertainty at the human level can undermine the prospects of effective nation-building just as uncertainty at the international level does. Thus we can see that the problems of political development are affected on the one side by international development and on the other by the state of individual psychology within the domestic society. In the light of these considerations it is useful to think of the problem of the underdeveloped areas as embracing a search for order at three levels, each of which may affect the stability of the others. Therefore national political development must occur in a context sensitive to both international or world currents and the psychological reactions of culturally uprooted peoples.

THE PRIOR ROLE OF ADMINISTRATION

Before moving completely to the present scene it is well to make another historical observation. We have noted that the continuous process of extending the nation-state system to all societies has involved three stages: (1) initial efforts to persuade traditional authorities to adhere to international standards, (2) colonial administration and foreign rule, and finally (3) indirect assistance and foreign aid. These three stages very roughly coincide with three others which reflect the different aspects of government that at different times were thought to be the most important in giving a society the critical qualities of a modern nation-state. These stages also represent the progressively deeper involvement of representatives of the international system in the domestic modernization process in transitional societies. Such involvement progressed from concern with the formal, surface qualities of the nation-state to an appreciation of the more fundamental political dynamics underlying the structure of the state.

During the first stage Europeans were uneasy about encountering societies which did not possess what they had come to accept as the kind of legal system essential to a modern nation.

---

chological Exploration (New Haven: Yale University Press, 1960); Margaret Mead, *Cultural Patterns and Technical Change* (Paris: UNESCO, 1953); O. Mannoni, *Prospero and Caliban: The Psychology of Colonization* (New York: Praeger, 1956).

Not only did they find intolerable the lack of standardized rules and regulations based upon universalistic considerations, but they also became convinced that the ultimate test of nationhood, and of membership in the community of modern states, depended upon the introduction of a Europeanized legal system. Thus the initial concept of political development focused upon the establishment of legal institutions. The introduction of extraterritoriality as demanded by the European powers in Turkey, China, Japan, and other countries of the non-Western world testifies to this preoccupation with legal institutions in building a modern state. In a very few cases the pressure of the international system for legal reforms was adequate to stimulate the development of modern nation-states.

In most situations, however, it became apparent that the transformation of traditional systems into nation-states would require more basic changes. Hence the second stage, when stress on a legal system was pushed to the point of establishing the machinery for the maintenance of law and order. Political development was assumed to coincide with administrative development — the characteristic rationale, of course, of colonialism.

We must pause to give special attention to this phase. It is of profound significance that the overriding stress in all Western efforts to make traditional societies into nations has been in the sphere of developing administrative capabilities. During the era of colonialism it was universally assumed that the process of political development involved primarily the creation and the effective operation of the authoritative instruments of the modern state. Whatever other motives were present, it was always believed that the highest expression of enlightenment was to be found in efforts to provide a society with efficient, competent, and rational administration. Political development meant the suppression of all irrationalities, emotionalisms, and wildly contending forces, in favor of coldly efficient, intelligent, and farsighted management of public affairs.

The notion that nation-building should properly follow up the development of competent administration remains in the philosophy behind much of the American foreign aid efforts.

In seeking to help others become nation-states Americans also have assumed that the heart of the problem lies not in the formalities of the legal system but in the realm of public administration and in the creation of a competent civil service. Both historically under colonialism and today through the weight of American aid programs the West has been overwhelmingly identified with efforts to strengthen the authoritative structures of government.

There is a great deal to justify this point of view, for certainly one of the distinctive characteristics of any developed political system is that it has greater capabilities or capacities than less developed systems. Modernization does imply a greater ability to deal effectively with a larger range of problems. The level of power available for policy choices is patently higher than in traditionally autocratic systems. And the key to greater capacity is the creation of modern administrative or bureaucratic structures. Hence historic stress upon administrative development was in response to the need of national political development.[10]

More recently, however, we have come to realize that civil administration, like the legal system, furnishes too narrow an approach to the task of nation-building. There is a more fundamental level of the nation-building process — the level of creating coherent political forces that can make meaningful a people's feeling of association with its polity. We are beginning to realize that, just as it was once necessary to go beyond the formalities of legal systems and build up administrative capabilities to maintain law and order and advance public policies, now it is necessary to go beyond instilling administrative skills and techniques and to strive at shaping the political context underlying formal governments.

BUILDING THE POLITICAL PROCESS

This history of attempts to make all societies into nation-states has been a long one, and it is important to have a clear

[10] For a general discussion of the central role of bureaucracy in political development see the essays in Joseph LaPalombara, ed., *Bureaucracy and Political Development* (Princeton: Princeton University Press, 1963).

sense of where we stand in this process. It is particularly important to realize that the West has long focused on the development of the administrative arts as a prerequisite to nation-building. We are only just beginning to realize that in the next stage in the development of a universalized nation-state system there is a far larger and more difficult task of developing political arts appropriate to nationhood.

Once the problem has been formulated in these terms, it becomes peculiarly disturbing to those who pride themselves on understanding that the informal is more fundamental in government to realize that historically the West has been mainly concerned with the formal structures of government. Indeed, to a degree that is puzzling in the light of modern political theory, we have left to chance the creation of the political bases of national politics.

This pattern of development suggests that the West has had an extraordinary faith in the powers of spontaneity in the building of nations. Basic to the most enlightened colonial policies was the expectation that if a people were given "good government," defined in administrative terms, they would eventually appreciate its wonders and develop automatically an intelligent political process that would fully support the essentials of rational administration. Likewise, American policies toward the ending of colonialism have been profoundly colored by the belief that once arbitrary and external restraints have been removed, a subjugated people will quite spontaneously develop democratic forms. We often feel that our kind of democracy is the most "natural" thing in the world and that, since we as a people are so inherently likeable, all others, if given the chance, will automatically emulate our ways.[11] Policy-wise all that we have felt to be necessary in assisting the newly independent countries has been to rectify the

11 We seem to be ambivalent on this score, and our alternative mood is one of appreciating our own uniqueness and thus feeling that no one else is really ready for, or capable of, truly democratic institutions. Thus we tend to vacillate between the pole of believing that others should be able to achieve democratic forms without the benefit of planning and programming and the pole of denying that others can or should ever really expect to make democracy work.

deficiencies of colonial policies. Thus we began the post-colonial epoch with the belief that marginal assistance, almost entirely in the realm of administration, should be enough to set the stage for the spontaneous development of democratic practices. Thus we began with Point Four, with technical assistance, and gradually we saw that the task called for more capital assistance; but now we are wondering whether we can ever be effective if we remain within the bounds of administrative programming.

It would be unjust to be overly critical of American policy-makers, for they have been remarkably quick to shed their preconceptions and to try to adjust to the demands of reality. The fault lies far more with the Western political theorists who have provided the ideas and concepts that have colored the vision of the policy-makers. Western political theory has given shockingly little attention to rational planning in building a democratic nation-state out of a traditional society, placing implicit faith in spontaneity as the prime dynamic factor in change and development.

In an even more fundamental sense modern political theory has encouraged a misplaced faith in spontaneity by its assumptions about the relationships between state and society, between formal institutions and informal patterns of behavior. A cardinal assumption of modern political science is that formal institutions are mere reflections of the fundamental values and cultural patterns of the society as a whole, and thus the kind of government a people will develop is determined by the general state of their society, their historical experience, and the interplay of contemporary social forces. This is a view that is quite inappropriate for understanding the evolution of institutions under Western impact and under the demands that they meet the standards of the nation-state system. These are societies in which the formal institutions of government have been introduced in a completely arbitrary fashion from the outside. At present most of the formal institutions of government throughout the non-Western world are not expressions of the particular values and cultures of the society. The structure, form, and operations of the modern nation-state are not "natural" prod-

ucts of most societies, but can develop only through the interactions of separate societies with the nation-state system operating as an external force.

To sum up, the process of nation-building in the new states
usually began with the establishment of the legal and administrative structures of modern government, but with little attention to how these might relate to political processes that would
make them responsive to political forces in the society. In most
cases every effort was made to isolate the operations of government from any contact with what might be considered potential political forces, and little attention was given to building
up political groups that might assume responsibility for determining the appropriate goals of administration while at the
same time respecting the integrity of the administrative system.

ADMINISTRATION VERSUS POLITICS

The great problem today in nation-building is that of relating the administrative and authoritative structures of government to political forces within the transitional societies. In
most ex-colonial countries there is an imbalance between recognized administrative tradition and a still inchoate political
process. In Vietnam and Pakistan, for example, power and authority are centered in the realm of administrative officialdom.
These administrative structures, which were built up during
the colonial period when governments were expected to rule
rather than to respond to political forces, have not been effectively transformed into agents of popular, representative politics.

It may not at first seem as though the same problem could
exist in countries where nationalist movements have over-
powered the colonial tradition of administrative rule and in
which politics unlimited seems sovereign. On closer examination, however, it becomes evident that even in such situations
there has been a gross imbalance between administrative traditions and political forces, and that the assault of the politicians
upon the administrative institutions is inspired by relative
weakness, not strength. Where they have, in a sense, had their
day of popular acceptance, nationalist movements have now

settled on the easy alternative of preserving their power by crowding in on the administrative structure rather than striving to build up permanent and autonomous bases of power. The leaders of such nationalist movements have tried to achieve their destiny by politicizing, and hence corrupting, the upper reaches of the administrative structures while allowing the mass base of their movements to wither and decline to the point that they can be used only to put on ritualistic demonstrations at times of "elections" or when foreign visitors need to be impressed. When the division between the administrative and the political is violated to such an extent, the capacity for effective administration declines and the development of political processes is also stifled.

The almost universal decline of political parties in the new states is evidence of the tendency of politicians to undermine the autonomy of administration rather than strengthen political representation. This weakening of the vitality and efficacy of political parties is in many respects the most ominous development in the post-colonial period. It is to be observed in countries that first seemed headed toward a multi-party system as well as in those which gained their independence under the auspices of a single nationalist movement. For example, Indonesia emerged from Dutch rule with a multiplicity of apparently vigorously contending and potentially coherent political parties that represented with reasonable accuracy the distribution of political interests and ideas of the country. Yet within a decade party politics is dead, administrative powers have been used to suppress some parties, and President Sukarno has even turned his back on building up his Nationalist Party in favor of ruling directly through the authoritative organs of government.[12] In other countries, such as Burma and Ghana, the dominant nationalist party that was the vehicle of the independence movement has lost its political significance as all the leaders have gradually sought the greater security and recognized authority that come from occupying a place in the administrative structures.

[12] Herbert Feith, *The Decline of Constitutional Democracy in Indonesia* (Ithaca: Cornell University Press, 1962).

The general conclusion is unmistakable. Nation-building in the new countries has encountered serious difficulties over the problem of establishing open politics outside of the sphere of administrative operations. Only in rare cases, such as in India, have the integrity of the civil service and the vitality of the political parties been maintained to a reasonable degree; and in India there are many disturbing signs of a decline in the autonomous strength of the Congress Party and of an excessive reliance upon administrative authority by Indian political leaders.[13] Elsewhere the general picture has been one of a decline in both the capacity to administer and the vitality of popular politics.

There is no denying the conspicuous decline in administrative effectiveness in many of the new countries. Our analysis suggests, however, that public administration cannot be greatly improved without a parallel strengthening of the representative political processes. In fact, excessive concentration on strengthening the administrative services may be self-defeating because it may lead only to a greater imbalance between the administrative and the political and hence to a greater need of the leaders to exploit politically the administrative services.

This is not the place to discuss the complex and extremely delicate interrelationships between administrator and politician, between instrumental technique and the selection of values and goals. It is sufficient to say that in any representative system, and indeed in any modern nation-state which depends upon applying technology to political purpose, these two functions and roles rarely rest in easy relationship with each other. Witness the history of relations between Congress and the Executive in the United States. In many respects the relationship in a parliamentary system is even more delicate, involving as it does the intimate but status-bound relations between Minister and Chief or Permanent Secretary. Yet clearly the problem is peculiarly acute in most transitional societies, where it constitutes a major obstacle to national development.

[13] Richard L. Park and Irene Tinker, eds., *Leadership and Political Institutions in India* (Princeton: Princeton University Press, 1959).

The main difficulty, as our historical analysis has suggested, is that the role of the administrator was created in almost complete isolation from that of the politician. To an extraordinary degree in most transitional societies the administrators and the politicians have developed quite separate traditions. More important, they have little tradition of working together and often harbor memories of intense conflicts during the last stages of the colonial period.[14] On the other hand, more stable patterns of development have occurred where the politician's role was created in conjunction with that of the administrator or where there was not an exaggerated building-up of the administrative services before the establishment of a public form of politics. For example, in India the Congress Party dates back to 1885, and the Indian politician and administrator had many opportunities to learn the importance of each other's roles before independence. Similarly, in the Philippines American administrators expected political parties to assume responsibilities almost as soon as the civil service was established.

It may be argued that we have possibly idealized the separate functions of bureaucratic management and political decision-making and that we have been thinking of bureaucracy in terms of a Weberian ideal type, ignoring the extent to which all administration involves an inherently political process. The query might be raised as to whether the administrative service might not be able to perform in many of these countries the functions left to political parties in the West. Viewed in such terms the degree to which the administrative services have been "politicized" should not be seen as a cause of concern but simply as a different way of arranging the political sphere.

Unfortunately we can take little comfort from such reasoning. We are not insisting that the new countries should respect

14 In many of the ex-colonial countries the administrative class has been viciously attacked by the nationalist politicians as a group of men who collaborated with the foreign rulers and worked against the nationalist movements. We shall return to this issue of loyalty and national identity in the struggle between administrator and politician; for a treatment with much greater detail about its manifestations in Burmese development see Lucian W. Pye, *Politics, Personality and Nation Building: Burma's Search for Identity* (New Haven: Yale University Press, 1962).

the division of powers that we have found useful, but rather that they need both effective administration and coherent political mobilization — and that they are tending to get neither. We are not suggesting that the administrative process should be devoid of politics. In many of the new countries administration would be far more effective if administrators were to adopt more aggressive measures and seek to be more political and less legalistic. Our point is only that the authoritative organs of government, weak as they are, tend to overshadow the non-bureaucratic components of the political system. Until these components have been strengthened, the new countries will have neither effective administration nor the bases for stable political processes.

SEPARATING THE PARTISAN AND THE NON-PARTISAN IN POLITICS

We turn now to an examination of the reasons for the relative weakness of the non-bureaucratic components of the political system. All the reasons for weakness that we shall be citing are related to one prime issue which rests at the heart of the nation-building problem in most new countries. This is the issue of the management of diversity and unity, more specifically the need to relate the parochial and the universal, to fuse basic components of the indigenous culture with the standards and practices of the modern world.

It is odd that the political class in most transitional societies fails to sense the legitimacy of the parochial in politics. Despite all the statements about the virtues of earlier traditions, the leaders of most transitional countries tend to feel intensely uneasy about any tradition-motivated group displaying political interests. Thus the validity of caste, of ethnic and linguistic groups, is denied, and it is assumed that nation-building can best proceed as though such differences did not exist. Parochial interests will not, however, disappear so easily, and in various ways they will intervene in the political process to haunt the nationalist politicians.[15]

[15] For a discussion of the function of interest articulation in the political process and of how interest articulation is performed in the develop-

The difficulty is that national leaders and those who would play the inner elite game of politics feel that they must represent the nation as a whole rather than particularistic interests. They feel that to build a modern nation they should suppress and inhibit anything that appears to be at odds with the ideal of a unified, modernized nation. In seeking to follow such a course the politicians risk representing no one but their own class. Even the administrator tends to have a clearer link with specific interests within the society. For in many transitional societies the administrators and government civil servants are identified with the people who were Westernized during the period of colonial rule. In this sense the administrators are spokesmen of a special interest group.

Indeed in many transitional societies the clash between administrator and politician has reinforced the politician's suspicions of particular interests and encouraged him to champion a diffuse and necessarily vague concept of the national interest. The politicians can sense that the higher civil service, though a potential modernizing agent, represents in fact the values, prejudices, and ambitions of a very definite and limited stratum of the total society — the more established, Westernized, and educated families. Generally the politicians do not belong to this social class, and they know that they cannot support it. Nor do they have a comparable social stratum of their own.

In other words, the emerging nationalist, and to a degree revolutionary, politicians of the new countries generally do not have strong ties with any particular segments of either the old, traditional society or the new, urbanized classes. In far too many countries the politicians at the national level lack links with the grass roots and the world of the peasant. In some cases they may find it essential to come to an accommodation with a landlord class, but this is usually not a happy or fruitful marriage. There may also be similar arrangements between politicians and individuals in the commercial and modern trading

ing countries see Gabriel A. Almond and James S. Coleman, eds., *The Politics of the Developing Areas* (Princeton: Princeton University Press, 1960).

world, but generally these are not regarded as legitimate associations designed to strengthen the society and the economy.[16]

The absence of concrete ways for fusing the parochial and the universal, the traditional and the modern, local sentiments and cosmopolitan standards, compels the politicians of many transitional societies to seek solutions by formulating ideological abstractions. A Sukarno feels compelled to talk about the need to rediscover the essence of Indonesian identity even as he undercuts the particular Indonesian groups engaged in advancing their collective identities. Many African politicians feel that they are representing the values and spirit of the parochial in their countries by turning their backs on the existing groups in their societies and joining with other politicians to search for the "soul of Africa" in the politics of "pan-African movements."

The fundamental problem of course is that in most transitional societies the process of social differentiation and specialization has not as yet reached the point of providing an adequate division of labor to give the basis for functionally specific interest groups. Yet at the same time the foundations for consensus in the traditional order have been so weakened that they are inadequate to support a new polity. In transitional societies many institutions are weak, but none are weaker than those that would articulate the diverse and competing interests of the society. The mechanisms for sifting out interests are so weak that national leaders feel compelled to act as though they were dealing with an essentially undifferentiated public.

Under these conditions politicians speak out in terms of the most general and abstract, avoiding the concrete or specific. They must seek to represent all by advancing ideologies that profess to encompass the interests of all; they must ask all the people to accept them as embodying the interests of the nation and hence the interests of all. This is the natural and easy strategy for politicians caught in such circumstances, but it is not a strategy which will foster stable representative institu-

16 For a discussion of the problem in the general context of all aspects of development see Max F. Millikan and Donald L. M. Blackmer, *The Emerging Nations* (Boston: Little, Brown, 1961).

tions. Democratic politics must be built upon a bargaining process in which the particular interests of all are respected and in which the politician seeks to perform a brokerage role in aggregating interests into various policy mixes.[17] Out of the tension between special and general interests arise both the dynamic basis for democratic politics and the fundamental consensus which molds diversity and flexibility into the unity and strength of a modern polity.

The inherent difficulty of relating the parochial and the cosmopolitan in most transitional societies creates within the political class a diffuse sense of distrust of all manifestations of assertive traditional life. It is here that we find the fundamental psychological source of the widespread anxiety of elites in underdeveloped societies that their countries will splinter apart over traditional communal differences. Objectively, many of these societies do have ethnic and language barriers dividing their peoples into different community groupings, and there is generally little consensus about the structure and form of the national political system. It seems, however, that in most of these countries these objective problems are greatly magnified by the politician's persisting belief that any acceptance of the parochial will invite disaster. More often than not the elite is only expressing fears of losing its own dominant position. Since it has identified its own well-being with the future of the country, it tends to see any threat to itself as a threat to the unity of the country.

By using the issue of national unity to prevent the representation of particularistic groupings, the political class generally weakens the coherence of the nation and produces tensions that in turn seem to justify authoritarian practices. In some instances the pattern is that of direct suppression of opposition elements and potentially dissident groupings, as for example in Ghana and Indonesia. In others the political elite has fallen

[17] On the theory of the bargaining process in democracy see Almond and Coleman, *op. cit.;* on the role of bargaining in a successfully developing country see Jean Grossholtz, *Politics in the Philippines* (Boston: Little, Brown, 1964).

back upon administrative rule and the inherent authority of the state apparatus.

Whenever the pressures of the parochial are too great, as for example in the agitation for linguistic states in India, and parochial interests have had to be accepted into the national political process, the result has usually been a strengthening of the national unity. In India it could be argued that most such concessions to linguistic groupings, castes, and other traditional associations have widened the range of people who have a satisfying sense of identification with the Union of India while at the same time weakening the partisan position of the Congress Party. It could be similarly maintained that in many Southeast Asian countries greater sensitivity on the part of the national elite for minority and regional interests might have reduced tensions and encouraged all groups to feel that they have a stake in the national government. It is equally clear that such concessions would have compromised the role of the particular elite group in power and weakened its claim of being the embodiment of the national interest.

This problem is closely related to the intensely politicized nature of social relations in most transitional societies. The political socialization process in most transitional societies has not instilled in people a strong sense for the distinction between the partisan and the impartial, between the political and the apolitical. In most such countries people have been trained to think about politics from an intensely partisan point of view and to reject the concept that there may be politically neutral and independent institutions. The struggle against colonialism and the morality of nationalist movements have generally taught people to see all politics as a struggle in which the gain of some is the loss for others. Such societies generally do not have the training in the nonpartisan civics common to the school system of modern states. Most do not believe in the possibility of an objective and politically neutral press, a professionalized system of mass communication, an independent judiciary, and a neutral civil service.

The American child is so politically socialized that he usually values and sees security in nonpartisan institutions and in ostensibly nonpartisan approaches to partisan politics.[18] He wants to accept the myth of an independent press and a non-political bureaucracy, and he tends to regard as cynical all suggestions that partisan considerations have affected these institutions. In contrast, the socialization process in most ex-colonial countries has instilled in the politically conscious the belief that virtue and security are to be found in a partisan point of view and that nothing in the realm of public affairs can or should be considered apolitical. We have already observed the practice of considering the civil service as representing a particular class of Westernized people. Usually the press is intimately associated with particular political groupings, and there are few significant public institutions which do not reflect the political coloration of the dominant group of politicians.

The absence of a strong feeling for the very realm of the nonpartisan and the apolitical means that people in transitional societies usually do not grasp such abstractions as the "national economy" or the "national polity." When all relations that go beyond the family, the village, and the immediately personal are seen as having a political dimension, it is difficult for people to appreciate the existence of distinct systems of social, political, and economic relations.

This problem is well illustrated by research experiences in Malaya and Burma, where it was discovered that many people who had been politically involved had little or no sense for such abstractions as a national "economy" or "polity." In their thinking, economic relations involved some people making profits at the expense of others, mainly merchants cheating customers; and political relations were seen largely as some people lording it over others. These people could not picture a neutral form of "economic development" that would improve all segments of a society. Many are therefore profoundly suspicious of the American claim of wanting to advance "economic development" in their country. In their view the only reality

[18] Herbert H. Hyman, *Political Socialization: A Study in the Psychology of Political Behavior* (Glencoe: The Free Press, 1959).

possible was for the United States to help some people get richer; and since they personally had no contacts with the Americans, they could only conclude that our aid was being given to others. On the other hand, the communist approach of supporting the workers and the peasants against the bourgeoisie and the imperialists conformed to the intensely partisan way in which most of these people see all political and social relationships.[19]

The lack of a strong sense of the impartial and the apolitical severely affects the security of the political class. In claiming a degree of legitimacy that extends beyond being merely a partisan political element many political elites seek to pose as national institutions essential for the well-being of the country as a whole. Thus although all relationships and all institutions tend to become highly politicized and there are relatively few politically independent structures in transitional societies, the constant effort of most dominant political elements is to deny the legitimacy of all competing political forces and to claim a position which is above, and not of, politics.

THE AVOIDANCE OF POLITICS

The lack of a clear separation between the realm of partisan issues and nonpartisan constitutional arrangements also means that in many transitional societies there is a fundamental denial of politics and an urge to suppress controversy. If we were to define "politics" as Bernard Crick does — "the activity by which differing interests within a given unit of rule are conciliated by giving them a share in power in proportion to their importance to the welfare and the survival of the whole community"[20] — then it would seem that in most new states there is a profound avoidance of politics.

This statement might seem to go against much of what we know about public life in these societies. What about the common observation that life in these countries has tended to be-

19 Lucian W. Pye, *Guerrilla Communism in Malaya: Its Social and Political Meaning* (Princeton: Princeton University Press, 1956).

20 Bernard Crick, *In Defense of Politics* (London: Weidenfeld & Nicolson, 1962, and Baltimore: Penguin Books, 1964) p. 21.

come intensely politicized since the days of nationalist movements? And what of Nkrumah's declaration, "Seek ye first the political heaven and then all else will follow," which has been so readily accepted in a host of new states? The point of course is that there has been a widespread recognition of the importance of power, the desirability of having authority, and the satisfactions of being able to use influence to gain advancement. But these approaches to the uses of power are not consonant with the concept of politics which goes back to Aristotle's view of the *polis* and a polity. Politics in this sense of the word means that the reality of controversy and the legitimacy of competition must be accepted and that a society is composed of differing interests that can be accommodated by the art of political adjustment and interaction.

In many of the new states politics is denied by stressing the need for consensus and a common ideology. Elsewhere the assertions of the monolithic demands of nationalism are used to suppress political competition. In still other countries the presumed requirements of a technocratic plan and the asserted need for rapid economic development are used to justify the denial of politics. The issues are complex, for it is far from clear whether empirically the suppression of politics does in fact facilitate the achievement of consensus, the vitalization of ideologies, the satisfaction of nationalism, or even the acceleration of economic activities. In any case, we shall want to return to these issues when we examine in greater detail the relationship of democracy to political development.

It is sufficient to note here, before turning to a discussion of the concept of political development, that historically the developing societies have not generally offered an environment conducive to the flourishing of politics as a process. Thus the leadership of many of these societies is frustrated by the fact, which Rousseau noted, that "the strongest is never strong enough to be always master unless he transforms strength into right and obedience into duty." The accent in many new states is still on strength and obedience.

CHAPTER II

The Concept of Political Development

THE SCHOLAR's world is always closer to the world of newspaper headlines than either scholars or laymen realize. The increasing academic interest in the problems of the new states in the process of political development has been inspired more by events in world politics than by any indigenous advances in political science theory. Thus, in large measure, the concept of political development was defined first by statesmen and policy-makers and not by scholars. The state of our current knowledge reflects this fact and so do the very words we use to discuss the problems of development.

The language of public policy is always in flux, for new concerns produce new terminologies. Yet in the language of politics, in which sloganeering is the common currency of presumed dialogues, fluency in the innovation of expressions rarely signals advancement in thought. At times fresh terms herald the awareness of novel problems, but more often they indicate merely frustration with intractable circumstances. When the language of politics seeks to define in broadest terms the contemporary human condition, it tends to be sensitive mainly to the emotions of hope, anxiety, or frustration that are inherent in the mind's erratic ability to either race ahead or fall far behind the tempo of substantive change. The political analyst in seeking the neutral ground of the observer inevitably faces the dilemma of being able neither to ignore popular terminology nor to use it effectively as the hard currency of disciplined intellectual exchange. And even if the analyst recognized that the qualities of ambiguity and imprecision which are virtues for the politician's art may be pitfalls for himself, he may still find himself the victim of a form of Gresham's law in political communication.

All this is of great relevance in trying to find meaning in current discussion of what is or should be happening in the poor and weak countries of the world. During the last decade the worldwide interest in the plight of these societies has produced a Babel of terms. Some of these express the aspirations of statesmen, others are the pompous pretensions of calculating politicians, and still others are merely the euphemisms of people who think that they may be talking about delicate matters. The result is that the study of the problems of these societies is so cluttered with loosely used terms that clear and disciplined communication has become difficult. We can observe how it has now become necessary to employ such optimistic and promiseful expressions as "developing" and "emergent" when discussing the gloomy cases of countries that are barely holding themselves together, whose governments are shaky and archaic, and whose peoples are growing faster in numbers than in well-being. The very terms of analysis suggest forecasts that may conflict with the predictions objective analysis is seeking to make.

To a large degree this state of semantic affairs can be explained by the fact that we are grappling with new problems of crisis dimensions, and when there is urgency there can rarely be order. The need is to get on with a job rather than tidy up language. Another way of characterizing the situation, however, is to say that scholars, who are the natural guardians of orderly thought and communications, were grossly unprepared for the demands of postwar history.

In the next chapter we shall have to examine some of the reasons why scholars were unprepared to handle many of the problems of conceptualizing the processes of political and social development. Before turning to this bit of intellectual history it will be helpful to separate all the various conflicting and overlapping notions and ideas commonly used in popular as well as professional interpretations of what is involved in political development. Although by now much of this confusion has subsided and there is a general acceptance of the importance of understanding the nature of political development, there is still considerable ambiguity and imprecision in the use of the mere term "political development."

DIVERSITY OF DEFINITIONS

It may therefore be helpful to elaborate some of the confusing meanings frequently associated with the expression "political development." Our purpose in doing so is not to establish or reject any particular definitions, but rather to illuminate a situation of semantic confusion which cannot help but impede the development of theory and becloud the purposes of public policy.

1. *Political Development as the Political Prerequisite of Economic Development.* When attention was first fixed on the problems of economic growth and the need to transform stagnant economies into dynamic ones with self-sustaining growth, the economists were quick to point out that political and social conditions could play a decisive role in impeding or facilitating advance in per capita income, and thus it was appropriate to conceive of political development, as the state of the polity which might facilitate economic growth.[1]

Operationally, however, such a view of political development tends to be essentially negative because it is easier to be precise about the ways in which performance of a political system may impede or prevent economic development than about how it can facilitate economic growth. This is true because his-

[1] Studies which in varying degrees take such an approach to political development include Paul A. Baran, *The Political Economy of Growth* (New York: Monthly Review Press, 1957); Norman S. Buchanan and Howard S. Ellis, *Approaches to Economic Development* (New York: The Twentieth Century Fund, 1955); Benjamin Higgins, *Economic Development: Principles, Problems and Policies* (New York: W. W. Norton, 1959); Albert O. Hirschman, *The Strategy of Economic Development* (New Haven: Yale University Press, 1958); Barbara Ward, *The Rich Nations and the Poor Nations* (London: Hamish Hamilton, 1962).

torically economic growth has taken place within a variety of political systems and with quite different ranges of public policies. This leads to the more serious objection that such a concept of political development does not focus on a common set of theoretical considerations, for in some cases it would mean no more than whether or not a government is following intelligent and economically rational policies, while in other situations it would involve far more fundamental considerations about the basic organization of the polity and the entire performance of the society. The problems of political development would thus vary according to particular economic problems in each country.

Another fundamental difficulty with such a view of political development has become increasingly apparent during the last decade as the prospects for rapid economic development have become exceedingly dim in many of the poor countries. Economies manifestly change far more slowly than political arrangements, and in many countries substantial economic growth — to say nothing of industrial development — is not likely in our generation although there may still be substantial political change and much that might, according to other concepts, seem to deserve the label of political development.[2]

Finally there is the objection that in most underdeveloped countries people clearly are concerned with far more than just material advancement; they are anxious about political development quite independent of its effects on the rate of economic growth. Therefore, to link political development solely to economic events would be to ignore much that is of dramatic importance in the developing countries.

  2. Political Development as the Politics Typical of Industrial Societies. A second common concept of political development, which is also closely tied to economic considerations, involves an abstract view of the typical kind of politics basic to already industrialized and economically highly advanced societies. The assumption is that industrial life produces a more-or-

2 See David Apter, "Steps Toward a Theory of Political Development," and "System, Process, and the Politics of Economic Development," both mimeo., n.d.

less common and generic type of political life which any society can seek to approximate whether it is in fact industrialized or not. In this view the industrial societies, whether democratic or not, set certain standards of political behavior and performance that constitute the state of political development and represent the appropriate goals of development for all other systems.[3]

The specific qualities of political development thus become certain patterns of presumably "rational" and "responsible" governmental behavior: an avoidance of reckless actions that threaten the vested interests of significant segments of the society, some sense of limitations to the sovereignty of politics, an appreciation of the values of orderly administrative and legal procedures, an acknowledgment that politics is rightfully a mechanism for solving problems and not an end in itself, a stress on welfare programs, and finally an acceptance of some form of mass participation.

3. Political Development as Political Modernization. The view that political development is the typical or idealized politics of industrial societies merges with the view that political development is synonymous with political modernization. The advanced industrial nations are the fashion-makers and pacesetters in most phases of social and economic life, and it is understandable that many people expect the same to be true in the political sphere. However, precisely the too easy acceptance of this view agitates the defenders of cultural relativism who question the propriety of identifying industrial — i.e., Western — practices as the contemporary and universal standards for all political systems.

Granting this objection, particularly when significance becomes attached to mere fad and fashion, it is still possible to discern in the movement of world history the emergence of certain conventions and even social norms that have increasingly been diffused throughout the world and that people gen-

[3] Walt W. Rostow emphasizes the relationship between stages of economic growth and forms of political organization in *The Stages of Economic Growth* (Cambridge: Cambridge University Press, 1960); and in *The Process of Economic Growth* (New York: W. W. Norton, 1952).

erally feel should be recognized by any self-respecting government. Many of these standards do trace back to the emergence of industrial society and the rise of science and technology, but most of them have by now a dynamic of their own. Mass participation, for example, reflects the sociological realities of industrialized life, but it also has been taken to be an absolute right in the spirit of current world views. Other ideals, such as the demand for universalistic laws, respect for merit rather than birth, and generalized concepts of justice and citizenship, seem now to hold a place above any particular culture and thus reasonably belong to some universal standards of modern political life.[4]

The question immediately arises as to what constitutes form and what is substance in this view of political development. Is the test of development the capacity of a country to equip itself with such modern cultural artifacts as political parties, civil and rational administrations, and legislative bodies? If so, then the matter of ethnocentrism may be of great relevance, for most of these institutions do have a peculiarly Western character. If, on the other hand, importance is attached only to the performance of certain substantive functions, then another difficulty arises because all political systems have historically, in one fashion or another, performed the essential functions expected of these modern *and* Western institutions. Thus, what is to distinguish between what is more and what is less "developed"? Clearly the problem of political development — when thought of as being simply political "modernization" — runs into the difficulty of differentiating between what is "Western"

[4] Several scholars have sought to compile indices of social and economic change and relate these to political and especially democratic development. See in particular James S. Coleman, "The Political Systems of the Developing Areas," in Gabriel A. Almond and James S. Coleman, eds., *The Politics of the Developing Areas* (Princeton: Princeton University Press, 1960); Seymour Martin Lipset, "Some Social Requisites of Democracy: Economic Development and Political Legitimacy," *American Political Science Review*, LIII, No. 1 (March 1959) 69-105; Karl W. Deutsch, "Social Mobilization and Political Development," *American Political Science Review*, Vol. LV, No. 3 (September 1961).

and what is "modern." Some additional criteria seem to be necessary if such a distinction is to be made.

   4. Political Development as the Operation of a Nation-State. To some degree these objections are met by the view that political development consists of the organization of political life and the performance of political functions in accordance with the standards expected of a modern nation-state. In this point of view there is an assumption that historically there have been many types of political systems and all communities have had their form of politics, but that with the emergence of the modern nation-state a specific set of requirements about politics came into existence. Thus, if a society is to perform as a modern state its political institutions and practices must adjust to these requirements of state performance. The politics of historic empires, of tribe and ethnic community, or of colony must give way to the politics necessary to produce an efficient nation-state which can operate effectively in a system of other nation-states.

Political development then becomes the process by which communities that are nation-states only in form and by international courtesy become nation-states in reality. Specifically, this involves the development of a capacity to maintain a certain level of public order, to mobilize resources for a specific range of collective enterprises, and to make and effectively uphold types of international commitments. The test of political development would thus involve, first, the establishment of a particular set of public institutions that constitute the necessary infrastructure of a nation-state, and, second, the controlled expression in political life of the phenomenon of nationalism. That is to say, political development is the politics of nationalism within the context of state institutions.[5]

   It is important to stress that from this point of view nation-

---

[5] This approach appears in K. H. Silvert, *Expectant Peoples: Nationalism and Development* (New York: Random House, 1964); Edward Shils, *Political Development in the New States* (The Hague: Mouton, 1962); and William McCord, *The Springtime of Freedom: Evolution of Developing Societies* (New York: Oxford University Press, 1965).

alism is only a necessary but far from sufficient condition to ensure political development. Development entails the translation of diffuse and unorganized sentiments of nationalism into a spirit of citizenship, and equally the creation of state institutions that can translate into policy and programs the aspirations of nationalism and citizenship. In brief, political development is nation-building.

5. *Political Development as Administrative and Legal Development.* If we divide nation-building into institution-building and citizenship development we have two very common concepts of political development. Indeed, the concept of political development as organization building has a long history, and it underlies the philosophy of much of the more enlightened colonial practices. For, as we have already observed in the history of the Western impact on the rest of the world, one of the central themes was the belief of Europeans that in building political communities it was essential to have, first, a legal order and then an administrative order.

This tradition has given great strength to current theories that the establishment of effective bureaucracies lies at the heart of the development process. In this view administrative development is associated with the spread of rationality, the strengthening of secular, legal concepts, and the elevation of technical and specialized knowledge in the direction of human affairs.[6]

Certainly no state can presume to be "developed" if it lacks completely the capacity to manage public affairs effectively, and wherever new states do have competent administrative institutions many problems are made manageable. On the other hand, as we observed in the first chapter, administration is not enough, and indeed when it is over-stressed it can create imbalances in the polity that may impede political development. In particular the concept of political development as merely

---

[6] Max Weber, *The Theory of Social and Economic Organization,* trans. by A. M. Henderson and Talcott Parsons (Glencoe: The Free Press, 1947); Joseph LaPalombara, ed., *Bureaucracy and Political Development* (Princeton: Princeton University Press, 1964).

improved administration overlooks entirely the problems of citizenship training and popular participation, both of which are clearly aspects of political development.

6. *Political Development as Mass Mobilization and Participation.* Another aspect of political development involves primarily the role of the citizenry and new standards of loyalty and involvement. Quite understandably, in some former colonial countries the dominant view of what constitutes political development is a form of political awakening whereby former subjects become active and committed citizens.

In some countries this view is carried to such an extreme that the effective and mass-demonstrational aspects of popular politics become an end in themselves, and leaders and citizens feel that they are advancing national development by the intensity and frequency of demonstrations of mass political passion. Conversely, some countries that are making orderly and effective progress may nevertheless be dissatisfied if they feel that their more demonstrative neighbors are experiencing greater "development." [7]

According to most views, political development does entail some degree of expanded popular participation, but it is important to distinguish among the conditions of such expansion. Historically in the West this dimension of political development was closely associated with the widening of suffrage and the induction of new elements of the population into the political process. This process of mass participation meant a diffusion of decision-making, and participation brought some influence on choice and decision. In some of the new states, however, mass participation has not been coupled with an electoral process but has been essentially a new form of mass response to elite manipulation. It should be recognized that even such limited participation has a role to play in nation-building since it

[7] See in particular Clifford Geertz, ed., *Old Societies and New States* (New York: Free Press of Glencoe, 1963); Rupert Emerson, *From Empire to Nation* (Cambridge: Harvard University Press, 1960); Bert F. Hoselitz, ed., *The Progress of Underdeveloped Areas* (Chicago: University of Chicago Press, 1952).

represents a means of creating new loyalties and a new feeling of national identity.[8]

Thus, although the process of mass participation is a legitimate part of political development, it is also fraught with the dangers of either sterile emotionalism or corrupting demagoguery, both of which can sap the strength of a society. The problem of course is the classic issue of balancing popular sentiments with public order; that is the fundamental problem of democracy.[9]

7. *Political Development as the Building of Democracy.* This brings us to the view that political development is or should be synonymous with the establishment of democratic institutions and practices. Certainly implicit in the view of many people is the assumption that the only form of political development worthy of the name is the building of democracies. Indeed, there are those who would make explicit this connection and suggest that development can have meaning only in terms of some form of ideology, whether democracy, communism, or totalitarianism. According to this view, development only has meaning in terms of the strengthening of some set of values, and to try to pretend that this is not the case is self-deceiving.[10]

As refreshing as it is to find examples of forthright and explicit identification of democracy with development, there is substantial resistance within the social sciences to such an ap-

[8] For a penetrating discussion of the problems of equality and citizenship in transitional societies see Lloyd Fallers, "Equality, Modernity, and Democracy in the New States," in Geertz, ed., *op. cit.;* S. N. Eisenstadt, "Breakdown of Modernization," *Economic Development and Cultural Change,* Vol. XII, No. 2 (July 1964); and Edward Shils, "The Concentration and Dispersion of Charisma: Their Bearing upon Economic Policy in Underdeveloped Countries," *World Politics,* Vol. XI, No. 1 (October 1958).

[9] Edward Shils, "Demagogues and Cadres in the Political Development of New States," in Lucian W. Pye, ed., *Communications and Political Development* (Princeton: Princeton University Press, 1963).

[10] For an excellent discussion of the relationship of democracy to development see Joseph LaPalombara, chapters I and II in LaPalombara, ed., *op. cit.*

proach. In part this is no doubt the result of a common aspiration within the social sciences to become a value-free science. Even when it is recognized that in an extreme form this aspiration is naive, there is still a sense of propriety which dictates that the categories of social science analysis should reflect reality rather than values.

Also, as a practical matter in the conduct of foreign aid policies, Americans have for interesting and revealing reasons believed, probably quite falsely, that it would be easier for us in our relations with underdeveloped countries to talk about "development" rather than "democracy." The argument in any case is that democracy is a value-laden term while development is more value-neutral. To use the building of democracy as the key to political development can thus be seen as an effort to push upon others American, or at least Western, values.

The problem of the relationship of democracy to political development is far too complex to be covered in this brief survey of attitudes, but since it is such an important issue, we shall devote a whole chapter to examining its various ramifications. In the meantime we need only note here that there are many people who would assert that development is fundamentally different from democracy, and that the very attempt to introduce democracy can be a positive liability to development.

8. Political Development as Stability and Orderly Change. Many of those who feel that democracy is inconsistent with rapid development conceive of development almost entirely in economic or social-order terms. The political component of such a view usually centers on the concept of political stability based on a capacity for purposeful and orderly change. Stability that is merely stagnation and an arbitrary support of the *status quo* is clearly not development except when its alternative is manifestly a worse state of affairs. Stability is, however, legitimately linked with the concept of development in that any form of economic and social advancement does generally depend upon an environment in which uncertainty has been reduced and planning based on reasonably safe predictions is possible.[11]

This view of development can be restricted mainly to the political sphere because a society in which the political process is capable of rationally and purposefully controlling and directing social change rather than merely responding to it is clearly more "developed" than one in which the political process is the hapless victim of social and economic "forces" that willy-nilly control the destiny of the people. Thus, just as some have argued that in modern societies man controls nature for his purpose while in traditional societies man sought mainly to adapt to nature's dictates, we can conceive of political development as depending upon a capacity to either control social change or be controlled by it. And of course the starting point in controlling social forces is the capacity to maintain order.

The problem with this view of development is that it leaves unanswered how much order is necessary or desirable and for what purpose change should be directed. There is also the question of whether the coupling of stability and change is not something that can occur only in the dreams of a middle class, or at least in societies that are far better off than most of the currently underdeveloped ones. Finally, on the scale of priorities there is the feeling that the maintenance of order, however desirable and even essential, stands second to getting things done; and thus development calls for a somewhat more positive view of action.[12]

9. Political Development as Mobilization and Power. The recognition that political systems should meet some test of performance and be of some utility to society leads us to the concept of political development as the degree of capability of a system. When it is argued that democracy may reduce the efficiency of a system, there is an implied assumption that it is

[11] For an extremely sophisticated and original interpretation of the relationship of order, control, and decision in social life see Karl W. Deutsch, *The Nerves of Government: Models of Political Communication and Control* (New York: Free Press of Glencoe, 1963).

[12] For an imaginative treatment of the relationship between stability and effective action see Fred W. Riggs, *Administration in Developing Countries* (Boston: Houghton Mifflin, 1964).

possible to measure the efficiency of a system, and in turn the notion of efficiency suggests theoretical or idealized models against which reality can be tested.

This point of view leads to the concept that political systems can be evaluated in terms of the level or degree of absolute power which the system is able to mobilize.[13] Some systems that may or may not be stable seem to operate with a very low margin of power, and the authoritative decision-makers are close to being impotent in their capacity to initiate and consummate policy objectives.[14] In other societies such decision-makers have at their command substantial power, and the society can therefore achieve a wider range of common goals. States naturally differ according to their inherent resource base, but the measure of development is the degree to which they are able to maximize and realize the full potential of their given resources.

It should be noted that this does not necessarily lead to a crude, authoritarian view of development as simply the capacity of a government to claim resources from the society. The capacity to mobilize and allocate resources is usually crucially affected by the popular support which the regime commands, and this is why democratic systems can often mobilize resources more efficiently than repressive authoritarian ones. Indeed, in practical terms the problem of achieving greater political development in many societies may involve primarily the realization of greater popular favor — not because of any absolute value of democracy but because only with such support can the system realize a higher degree of mobilization of power.

When political development is conceived of in terms of mo-

[13] For the analysis of the concept of capacity as basic to political development see James S. Coleman, "The Development Syndrome," in the forthcoming final volume of the Social Science Research Council's Committee on Comparative Politics' Series in Political Development to be published by the Princeton University Press. Also see Talcott Parsons, "Evolutionary Universals in Society," *American Sociological Review*, Vol. XXVII (June 1964); Gabriel A. Almond, "Political Systems and Political Change," *The American Behavioral Scientist*, Vol. VI (June 1963).

[14] For the impotencies of developing systems see Eisenstadt, "Breakdown of Modernization," *op. cit.*

bilization and an increase in the absolute level of power in the society, it becomes possible to distinguish both a purpose for development and also a range of characteristics associated with development. Many of these characteristics in turn can be measured, and hence it is possible to construct indices of development. Items in such indices might include prevalence and penetration of the mass media measured in terms of newspaper circulation and distribution of radios, the tax basis of the society, the proportion of population in government and their distribution in various categories of activities, the proportion of resources allocated to education, defense, and social welfare.[15]

10. *Political Development as One Aspect of a Multi-Dimensional Process of Social Change.* The obvious need for theoretical assumptions to guide the selection of the items that should appear in any index for measuring development leads us to the view that political development is somehow intimately associated with other aspects of social and economic change.[16] This is true because any item that may be relevant in explaining the power potential of a country must also reflect the state of the economy and the social order. The argument can be advanced that it is unnecessary and inappropriate to try to isolate too completely political development from other forms of development. Although to a limited extent the political sphere may be autonomous from the rest of society, for sustained political development to take place it can only be within the context of a multi-dimensional process of social change in which no segment or dimension of the society can long lag behind.

According to this point of view all forms of development are related, development is much the same as modernization, and it takes place within a historical context in which influences

[15] For a detailed listing of the indices of mobilization see Deutsch, "Social Mobilization and Political Development," *op. cit.*

[16] This is the approach underlying Max F. Millikan and Donald L. M. Blackmer, *The Emerging Nations* (Boston: Little, Brown, 1961). See also Daniel Lerner, *The Passing of Traditional Society* (New York: Free Press of Glencoe, 1958).

from outside the society impinge on the processes of social change just as changes in the different aspects of a society — the economy, the polity, and the social order — all impinge on each other.

THE DEVELOPMENT SYNDROME

There are other possible interpretations of political development — for example, the view common in many former colonies that development means a sense of national self-respect and dignity in international affairs, or the view more common in advanced societies that political development should refer to a post-nationalism era when nation-state will no longer be the basic unit of political life. And it would also be possible to distinguish other variations on the theme that we have just presented. For our purposes we have gone far enough to point out, first, the degree of confusion that exists with the term political development, and, second, the extent to which, behind this confusion, there does seem to be a certain more solid basis of agreement. Without trying to assert any particular philosophical orientation or theoretical framework, it may be useful to scan the various definitions or points of view just reviewed in order to isolate those characteristics of political development which seem to be most widely held and most fundamental in the general thinking about problems of development.[17]

The first broadly shared characteristic noted is a general spirit or attitude toward *equality*. In most views on the subject, political development does involve mass participation and popular involvement in political activities. Participation may be either democratic or a form of totalitarian mobilization,

[17] The specific themes which follow, relating to the "development syndrome," were identified by members of the Comparative Politics Committee of the Social Science Research Council and they will be elaborated upon in much greater detail in James S. Coleman's contribution to the final volume of the Committee's Series in Political Development to be published. The remaining paragraphs of this chapter merely summarize the work of several members of the Committee, including in particular Leonard Binder, James S. Coleman, Joseph LaPalombara, and Myron Weiner.

but the key consideration is that subjects should become active citizens, and at least the pretenses of popular rule are necessary.

Equality also means that laws should be of a universalistic nature, applicable to all and more or less impersonal in their operation. Most often this has meant the development of a codified legal system and explicit legal procedures. The critical consideration, however, is the recognition that all people, whether rich or poor, strong or weak, should submit to the same dictates of law.

Finally, equality means that recruitment to political office should reflect achievement standards of performance and not the ascriptive considerations of a traditional social system. The assumption in a developed political system is that people must have displayed appropriate merit to gain public office and that officeholders should have met some competitive test of competence.

A second major theme we find in most concepts of political development deals with the *capacity* of a political system. In a sense, capacity is related to the outputs of a political system and the extent to which the political system can affect the rest of the society and economy. Capacity is also closely associated with governmental performance and the conditions that affect such performance.

More specifically, capacity entails first of all the sheer magnitude, scope, and scale of political and governmental performance. Developed systems are presumed to be able to do a lot more and touch upon a far wider variety of social life than less developed systems can. In a sense, with development government moves from the stage of being a social preoccupation to becoming an industry.

Second, capacity means effectiveness and efficiency in the execution of public policy. Developed systems, presumably, not only do more things than others but also do them faster and with much greater thoroughness. There is thus a trend toward professionalization of government. Concern with efficiency and effectiveness leads also to universally recognized standards of performance.

Finally, capacity is related to rationality in administration and a secular orientation toward policy. Government's actions are guided more by deliberations and justifications that seek to relate ends and means in a systematic manner. Planning becomes possible.

A third theme running through much of the discussion of political development is that of *differentiation* and specialization.[18] This is particularly true in the analysis of institutions and structures. Thus this aspect of development involves first of all the differentiation and specialization of structures. Offices and agencies tend to have their distinct and limited functions, and there is an equivalent of a division of labor within the realm of government.

With differentiation there is, of course, increased functional specificity of the various political roles within the system. And, finally, differentiation also involves the integration of complex structures and processes. That is, differentiation is not fragmentation and the isolation of the different parts of the political system but specialization based on an ultimate sense of integration.

In recognizing these three dimensions of equality, capacity, and differentiation as lying at the heart of the development process we do not mean to suggest that they necessarily fit easily together. On the contrary, historically the tendency has usually been that there are acute tensions between the demands for equality, the requirements for capacity, and the processes of greater differentiation. Pressure for greater equality can challenge the capacity of the system, and differentiation can reduce equality by stressing the importance of quality and specialized knowledge.

Indeed, it may in fact be possible to distinguish different patterns of development according to the sequential order in

[18] The concept of differentiation in relationship to political development is analyzed in S. N. Eisenstadt, "Social Change, Differentiation, and Evolution," *American Sociological Review,* Vol. 29 (June 1964); Neil J. Smelser, "Mechanisms of Change and Adjustment to Change," in Bert F. Hoselitz and Wilbert E. Moore, eds., *Industrialization and Society* (The Hague: UNESCO, Mouton, 1963).

which different societies have dealt with the different aspects of the development syndrome. In this sense development is clearly not unilinear nor is it governed by sharp and distinct stages, but rather by a range of problems that may arise separately or concurrently. In seeking to pattern these different courses of development and to analyze the different types of problems it is useful to note that the problems of equality are generally related to the *political culture* and sentiments about legitimacy and commitment to the system; the problems of capacity are generally related to the performance of the *authoritative* structures of government; and the questions of differentiation touch mainly on the performance of the *non-authoritative* structures and the general political process in the society at large. This suggests that in the last analysis the problems of political development revolve around the relationships between the political culture, the authoritative structures, and the general political process.

CHAPTER III

The Need for Theory

I N NOTING the confusion which exists over the concept of political development we have pointed to the need for fuller
theories of nation-building, and we have also suggested the
danger that can arise from faulty conceptualization. Without
theories that reflect the realities of history we have no standards for judging performance in any particular situation.
What can reasonably be expected of new governments? What
patterns of behavior can be accepted as normal and appropriate, and what should be judged as pathological? If we should
not apply to transitional societies the same criteria we do to
evaluating developed and more long-standing systems, then
what principles should we use? And if we were to commit ourselves to inappropriate theories, we might arrive at grossly unrealistic expectations about what can be accomplished in a
short time and with inadequate policies.

The lack of doctrine prevents us from providing helpful interpretations about the significance of various trends and tendencies common to transitional societies.[1] Is the emergence of
army rule a sign of anti-democratic tendencies? Or is it a process that can be readily expected at particular stages of national

1 For a more complete analysis of the need for a doctrine of democratic
development, and one upon which this discussion leans heavily, see Lucian
W. Pye, *Politics, Personality, and Nation Building* (New Haven: Yale University Press, 1962) chapter 1.

development? Must the central government try to obliterate all traditional communal differences, or can the unfettered organization and representation of conflicting interests produce ultimately a stronger sense of national unity? Should the new governments strive to maintain the same levels of administrative efficiency as the former colonial authorities did, or is it possible that because administration was the prime justification for the legitimacy of the colonial rule and because the new governments have other claims of legitimacy, this is no longer as crucial a problem? The questions mount, and we are not sure which trends are dangerous and which are only temporary phases with little significance.

The lack of doctrine has paralyzed constructive criticism and permitted the political dialogue in the new countries to become mired down in cant. Without the reassurance of meaningful standards of appraisal for evaluating behavior, people will feel incapable of exposing politics to the benefits of rigorous tests of judgments. Whenever people feel inhibited in discussing the realities of politics and seek to rationalize the need for optimistic fictions the danger increases, so that even common varieties of political skulduggery will become immune to attack. Foreigners and men of good will can then innocently protect the work of rogues, while those who are inside become cynical about the judgment of those who would wish well of such societies. For example, in the absence of a doctrine for democratic development little can be done to oppose the perverse notion that somehow democracy can be equated with inefficiency, incompetence, and administrative slovenliness, while totalitarian methods are equated with efficiency, intelligence, and steadfastness of purpose. Leaders of new countries have been able to rationalize all manner of human failings as manifestations of their commitment to the democratic approach and thus claim virtues for their follies.

Before turning to the main traditions of scholarship which have proved to be most helpful in shedding light on the processes of political development, it is relevant to note some of the reasons why the social sciences were unprepared to provide the knowledge necessary for guiding strategies of national development. Our purpose is not to seek the presumed benefits of self-criticism, but rather to point to some intellectual considerations which may still interfere with clear thinking about political development either as a theoretical concept or as a practical objective of policy.

From the perspective of intellectual history it is striking that the issue of development in its economic, social, and political guises arose to challenge the social scientists just at the time when we thought we had buried the presumably old-fashioned and innocent concept of progress. Although earlier social theorists had certainly given support to the notion of human progress and social evolution, modern social scientists have generally been somewhat embarrassed by this popular Western and peculiarly American article of faith. With the rise of the dictators and the holocaust of World War II, the mood of social science was at best agnostic and skeptical to any suggestion about either the inevitability or even the desirability of progress. With this as background, the social sciences were hardly ready to embrace enthusiastically the concept of "development" as applied to the non-Western world. Consequently we have had to go through a period of adjustment during which there has been some suspicion that the presumably discredited notion of progress was again appearing through a back door. The problem has certainly created some intellectual confusion and has diverted some energies into marginal and unproductive skirmishes.

In a nearer perspective of intellectual history the question of development caught the social sciences at the high point in our belief in cultural relativism. Although World War II had raised some question about the validity of dispensing tolerance towards all cultures, certainly the mainstream of social science favored the spirit of accepting the propriety of cultural differences and of respecting the realities of contemporary life in every society. In countering the evils of enthnocentrism rather strong taboos were erected against even implying that some societies might be more "advanced" or more "developed" than others. This meant that general standards of social and political performance were out, and behavior in one society should not be judged against performance in another.

In the light of this development it came as a shock to doctrinaire champions of cultural relativism to discover that their doctrines could be cruelly degrading precisely to those to whom it was intended to give respectability. For, when crudely put, the concept of cultural relativism could be read to mean that it was in the nature of some societies to be rich and powerful and for others to be poor and ineffectual. The doctrine could easily be misunderstood as a balm to the poor to make it possible for them to rationalize their lot.

Aside from this, misunderstanding the ethic of cultural relativism has impeded thought about the problems of development because it has left the social scientists unsure as to whether they should properly be concerned with assisting others to change their ways and deviate from their heritages. To be concerned with development can all too often seem the same as trying to make others over into the image of ourselves as long as it is accepted that we are somehow more developed than they are. The very legitimacy of development is thus brought into question by the spirit of cultural relativism. It is not our purpose to dwell on these issues of propriety except to point out that the manifest urgency of the historical problem of development has in the main forced social scientists to suppress some of their scruples of cultural relativism but has left them without strong philosophical underpinnings to support their involvement in the development problems.

The emergence of the problems of development also caught political science at a time when the discipline thought that it was successfully breaking from its earlier and strongly normative tradition. Modern political science, in seeking to become an empirical discipline, has been anxious to be highly realistic and to deal with conditions and processes as they actually occur in life. This fundamental trend again seems in some respects to conflict with the orientations necessary for working on the problems of development; for if development means anything, it means a rejection of current realities in favor of hoped-for eventualities. The spirit of empiricism, in replacing interest in utopias and in more ideal arrangements, had given a certain sense of legitimacy to the ongoing workings of any political process, which in turn had left political scientists with the feeling that reformism was slightly naive and that change and improvement could only be incremental. This outlook on history was hardly calculated to be of help and encouragement to the leaders and intellectuals of new states impatient for dramatic change.

In addition to dominant trends in the philosophic orientations of the social sciences the recently fashionable operating procedures and methodologies have also limited our ability to deal with the problems of development. Briefly, after World War II the social sciences felt that they were coming of age as sciences, and thus they tended to place a high value on precision, rigor, and exactness of measurement, qualities which are all more compatible with systematic but essentially static modes of analysis. Our awareness of the possibilities of sophisticated techniques of investigation has made us uncomfortable with loose and broad generalizations. With our methodological sophistication we have also come to appreciate fully the intellectual reasons why dynamic modes of analysis, so essential for understanding the development process, are inherently far more difficult and to some degree beyond our current capabilities if the highest standards of rigor are to be maintained. Although fortunately many social scientists have been prepared to meet the challenge of work in the imperfect research environments of the new states, they have had to risk criticism that their work was not up to the levels of exactness now expected of studies in our own society.

There have of course always been social scientists accustomed to studying foreign societies without being inhibited by the difficulties of research rigor. Yet even this tradition has not proved to be ideal preparation for conceptualizing the problems of development. The emphasis of anthropology and foreign-area studies has been largely in terms of the concept of culture, for in the past the prime intellectual challenge was to explain the uniqueness of different societies and the persistence of historical traditions. The provocative question was how to explain continuity and the persistence of cultural patterns, and not social change. Consequently, those who have worked most closely with the concept of culture and who have known foreign cultures most intimately have tended to be primarily sensitive to the limitations of rapid change and the inhibitions to effective development.

The real problems of economic and political development in the new states have suddenly made us realize that we had never actually resolved the issues between the concept of social evolution and the principles of cultural relativism. We had only pushed them into the background.* We realize now that we have been living with both; at some moments we have been cultural relativists, and at other times we have found it more convenient to talk in terms of evolution, growth, stages of development, and other such concepts inherent in the view of social progress.

The dilemma posed by the issue of evolution versus cultural relativism is made more acute by the ability of the economists to rank different countries according to indices of relative development that suggest an essentially unilinear concept of progress. If we can so readily speak of stages of economic development, why shouldn't we be able to do the same with political development? Indeed, as we learn more about the dynamics of economic development it becomes increasingly apparent that the conditions of economic growth are closely linked to cultural attitudes and political practices, and hence economic development cannot be independent of political and cultural development.

However, once the problem is pushed to this point, we are confronted with the issue of what should be taken as the criteria of political development. And once these issues of values are raised, the pull of cultural relativism becomes overpowering. Who is to say what state of social affairs is more

---

* The remaining paragraphs in this section first appeared in Lucian W. Pye, "Democracy, Modernization, and Nation Building," in J. Roland Pennock, ed., *Self-government in Modernizing Nations*. © 1964. By permission of Prentice-Hall, Inc., Englewood Cliffs, N.J.

advanced or more retarded? And we are quickly back to all the doubts about the appropriateness of applying concepts of progress, development, and modernization to the political sphere.

The clash between evolutionary theory and cultural relativism is a basic one and cannot be easily sidestepped. At the same time, however, it does seem possible to recognize that to a considerable degree we can surmount the difficulty if we alter the historical and analytical perspectives from which we customarily approach the problems of political development.

The issue of evolution versus cultural relativism is most acute when we think in terms of a world composed of more or less autonomous political systems. Unfortunately this has been the fundamental outlook basic to most contemporary social science. In comparative politics, for example, we have tended to analyze countries as though they were relatively isolated and independent political systems with their own inner dynamics. Once the problem of change is posed in these terms, we are compelled to search for law-like propositions which might describe the change, "growth," and "development" of such systems. At the same time we also are compelled by this approach to respect the unique configurations of each particular system. It is therefore precisely a consequence of our thinking of societies as relatively autonomous systems that we are confronted with the frustrating issue of the search for evolutionary "laws" and the appreciation of cultural uniqueness.

The historical facts suggest, however, that change is generally not a problem basic to separate and relatively autonomous systems but one overwhelmingly related to interactions among systems. Social change can in many ways be generated by isolated social systems, but the historical set of major changes that we are concerned about when speaking of the problems of the new states is clearly a function of cultural diffusion. In particular when we treat the problems of nation-building it is not appropriate to think of a world of autonomous systems each developing, growing, and maturing according to some fundamental laws of organic change and evolution. Nation-building in the present age is taking place in a world in which powerful international currents are pushing the various societies in roughly the same direction.

It is useful at this point to quote at some length the anthropologist Robert H. Lowie at the conclusion of his classic study of social organization, *Primitive Society:*

> The belief in social progress was a natural accompaniment of the belief in historical laws, especially when tinged with the evolutionary optimism of the 'seventies of the nineteenth century. If inherent necessity urges all societies along a fixed path, metaphysicians may still dispute whether the underlying force be divine or diabolic, but there can at least be no doubt as to which community is retarded and which accelerated in its movement toward the appointed goal. But no such necessity or design appears from the study of culture history. Cultures develop mainly through the borrowings due to chance contact. Our own civilization is even more largely than the rest a complex of borrowed traits. The singular order of events by which it has come into being provides no schedule for the itinerary of alien cultures. Hence the specious plea that a given people must pass through such or such a stage in *our* history before attaining this or that destination can no longer be sustained.[2]

Lowie reminds us also of the profound words of the jurist Maitland in *Domesday Book and Beyond,* which he quotes:

> Even had our anthropologists at their command material that would justify them in prescribing that every independent portion of mankind must, if it is to move at all, move through one fated series of stages which may be designated as Stage A, Stage B, Stage C, and so forth, we still should have to face the fact that the rapidly progressive groups have been just those which have not been independent, which have not worked out their own salvation, but have appropriated alien ideas and have thus been enabled, for anything that we can tell, to leap from Stage A to Stage X without passing through any intermediate stages. Our Anglo-Saxon ancestors did not arrive at the alphabet or at the Nicene Creed by traversing a long series of "stages"; they leapt to the one and to the other.[3]

[2] Originally published in 1920 by Horace Liveright, *Primitive Society* was reprinted by Harper Torchbooks (New York: 1961); see pp. 440-41.

[3] *Ibid.*, p. 435.

It does seem possible that the present-day tensions of international politics, the spectacular material success of the industrial societies, and the ever-increasing pressures of expanding populations in backward countries may be combining to create a special historical and temporal form of "inherent necessity" which Lowie did not feel at his time of writing but which has become a powerful force in contemporary world politics. This form of "necessity" which can appear only in the form of political demands and pressures does not change the inherent nature of societies nor does it justify our thinking of societies as being governed by specific and universal laws of growth. Indeed, there is considerable danger that in the light of the pressing policy problems of development in the new states people will come to think increasingly of all human societies as organic entities with very definite patterns of growth. This is especially likely to be the case as we tend more and more to apply shorthand terminology to different ranges of policy problems and thus to speak of country A as being at such and such a stage of development and country B at another stage. If we are to use such terminology, we must constantly remind ourselves that we have no solid intellectual grounds to justify the notion that all societies must or are likely to pass through discernible and historically progressive stages of evolution.

It is true that many respected philosophers of history and students of civilization have postulated that societies have life cycles which follow discernible laws. Basic to the thinking of such different men as Marx, Toynbee, and Spengler has been a common effort to elucidate the sequences of growth, development, and decline of human societies. And certainly the founders of modern sociology were intensely interested in the problem of social evolution. Max Weber, in seeking to explain the industrial revolution in Europe, formulated the evolutionary patterns of changes in forms of authority in which the traditional system gave way to the charismatic, and then, if development continued, the rational-legal form of authority would emerge.[4] Auguste Comte also formulated a three-stage progres-

[4] Max Weber, *The Theory of Social and Economic Organization*, trans. by A. M. Henderson and Talcott Parsons (Glencoe: The Free Press, 1947).

sion of social evolution: the theological, the metaphysical, and the positivist periods.[5] And of course many others have sought to find some historical order in the experiences of societies and civilizations. For our purposes it is not necessary to evaluate all of these efforts; it is sufficient to recognize that these authors have been dealing with units of human history that are far larger both in terms of cultural areas and historical time than the relatively modest units represented by the new states of the underdeveloped areas. Whatever the merits of any particular theory about the rise and fall of civilizations, they are not likely to be manifest when applied to the situation in the various new states of the contemporary underdeveloped world.

THE CONTRIBUTIONS OF SOCIAL THEORISTS [6]

There has generally been greater intellectual precision in the efforts of the social theorists who have sought to explain the industrial revolution and to characterize the essential differences between social relations in a traditional community and those in a modern society. These thinkers have suggested that it is possible to conceive of all societies as being divided into two general groupings. There has been a host of labels for the two categories, each designation emphasizing different elements of the typologies: traditional and rational, rural and urban, agricultural and industrial, primitive and civilized, static and dynamic, sacred and secular, folk and urban, *societa* and *civitas*, *Gemeinschaft* and *Gesellschaft*, communal and associational, traditional and modern. What these social theorists have done is to create composite pictures of all traditional societies on the one hand and of all modern societies on the other; then they have selected from among the thousand and one differences between the two those key characteristics which they feel are the most significant in explaining the gross differences between them.

As early as 1861 Sir Henry Maine identified the two types of

[5] Auguste Comte, *The Positive Philosophy*, trans. by Harriet Martineau (London: George Bell & Sons, 1896).

[6] This section reproduces the discussion which appeared in Pye, *op. cit.*, chapter 3.

societies and postulated that all progress involved a movement from the "status" to the "contract" type.[7] Maine noted that a status society was characterized largely by the assignment of individual rights and duties on the basis of familial and kinship considerations, and that the tone of such societies was set by the awareness of individuals of the special and particular bonds that each had with each other. On the other hand, a contract society was based upon territorial ties, and individuals were bound to each other by secular, contractual relationships based upon specific considerations but enforced by the acceptance of a universally defined standard of ethics. In arguing that the development of societies involved the transition from tradition-bound, status-oriented relationships to rationally calculated and contractually negotiated relationships Maine summed up the essential elements of what is a century later still the dominant social science view of the question.

Taking Maine's thesis as a point of departure, Ferdinand Toennies in 1887 made a further advance in his *Gemeinschaft und Gesellschaft*[8] by noting that human relations in the *Gemeinschaft* (community) form of association were highly affective, emphasizing the nonrational, emotional dimensions of the "natural will" of man that have their clearest expressions in the intimate feelings of kinship, comradeship, and neighborliness, while relations in the *Gesellschaft* (society) form of association were effectively neutral and emphasized the rational capacities of man by which he is able, first, to isolate and distinguish his goals of action, and then to employ, impersonally and deliberately, contractual arrangements as a part of strategies for optimizing his values. Thus Toennies stressed the distinction between the affective, emotion-based communal society in which everyone had a sense of belonging and the effectively neutral relationships of the modern society in which

[7] Henry Maine, *Ancient Law: Its Connection with the Early History of Society and Its Relation to Modern Ideas* (London: Lardon J. Murray, 1861).

[8] Ferdinand Toennies, *Gemeinschaft und Gesellschaft* (1887), trans. by Charles P. Loomis, *Fundamental Concepts of Sociology* (New York: American Book Co., 1940).

each individual builds his relations with others out of the ends-means calculations which guide his quest for his individual goals.

With both Maine and Toennies there was an acceptance of progress, but not without a note of nostalgia for the comfortable relationships of traditional societies and some anxiety over the prospects of a chillingly impersonal and ruthlessly calculating modern society. It is therefore noteworthy that Emile Durkheim, the father of modern sociology, in advancing his dichotomous scheme in 1893, not only stressed the virtues of the advanced form of social relationships but also employed odd and seemingly reversed labels for his two categories of social solidarity.[9] He characterized the traditional order as having a "mechanical" form of solidarity that was based on the sharing of common attitudes and sentiment and in which legal authority had to be "repressive." In contrast "organic solidarity" was the basis of the advanced society, with its highly specialized division of labor in which interests and sentiments differed but were mutually complementary and hence legal authority was "restitutive." Instead of the class struggle of Marx, Durkheim saw the diversity of the modern plural society as providing the individual with unlimited opportunities for self-development and the expression of individual genius. A central contribution of Durkheim to any theory of nation-building was the proposition that a national consensus built on merely a common set of shared values would always be more fragile and more open to authoritarian rule than one built on the need to aggregate the diverse but intensely real interests of all the elements of a society. Durkheim thus pointed to the fundamental importance of social roles and their relationships in the development of the modern and more complex society, and to the fact that the differentiation of roles increases rather than decreases the solidarity of a society.

It remained for Max Weber, however, to bring together the strands in the tradition of dichotomous schemes of social de-

[9] Emile Durkheim, *De la Division du travail social* (1893), trans. by George Simpson, *The Division of Labor in Society* (Glencoe: The Free Press, 1949).

velopment.[10] In addition to elaborating, with great erudition and profound historical insight, the distinctive qualities of the traditional and the rational-legal forms of authority, Weber also identified the charismatic form of authority with its emphasis upon the affectual type of social action. In doing so he brought to light a transitional form of society and pointed out the qualities of social action that tend to predominate when traditional forms are weakened. It would be hard to overemphasize Weber's contribution in developing his typologies of authority and social action. But probably an even greater contribution was his suggestion that there is an inner coherence to all societies in the form of a systematic relationship among the social, economic, legal, and political forms of behavior on the one hand, and the nonrational spirit or ethos of the society, as best expressed in its religion, on the other. His successes in relating the rise of the rationalistic institutions of capitalism to the ascetic character of Calvinism led him to explore the relationship of the main religions of the East to the secular institutions they fostered. Through such endeavors Weber cleared the scene for a systematic analysis of the relationships between objective social forms and the subjective, psychological meaning of behavior. The social, economic, and political realms were seen as no more than different aspects of basic human acts, all conditioned and given coherence by the psychological makeup of man. Weber thus set the stage for relating questions of social structure to the profound psychological insights of Freud.

Using the central concepts of Max Weber as a point of departure, Talcott Parsons has brought about a higher degree of precision by relating the types of social action to the theory of role relationships and by identifying certain key "pattern vari-

[10] A useful introduction to Weber's thinking on the problems of social change is to be found in Reinhard Bendix, *Max Weber: An Intellectual Portrait* (New York: Doubleday, 1960). The most pertinent parts of Weber's writing for the problems of nation-building are to be found in translation in *The Theory of Social and Economic Organization, op. cit.; From Max Weber: Essays in Sociology,* trans. by Hans Gerth and C. Wright Mills (New York: Oxford University Press, 1946); *The Protestant Ethic and the Spirit of Capitalism,* trans. by Talcott Parsons (New York: Scribner, 1930; paperbound, 1958).

ables." [11] In brief, Parsons noted that in the traditional society status rested upon *ascriptive* considerations while in the modern society *achievement* standards predominate, that in the traditional system role relationships tended to be functionally *diffuse* in the sense that all aspects of behavior may be considered relevant to any relationship, while in the modern system relationships tend to be functionally *specific* in the sense that they are limited only to the essential considerations relevant for maintaining the effectiveness of the system. Also, in the traditional system the normative basis of relationships was *particularistic* considerations and not the *universalistic* ones of the modern society. Others have followed Parson's lead and have sought either to make the key distinctions more logically rigorous or to construct conceptual models of political systems based upon them.[12] Parsons, however, must be personally credited with significantly advancing the discussion of the differences between traditional and modern social orders, and his pattern variables have been widely accepted by contemporary social scientists as illuminating the crucial differences between the two.

CRISES IN POLITICAL DEVELOPMENT

The focus of the social theorist which we have just reviewed is on the differences in types of societies and not on the dynamics of change or transition. For purposes of political analysis it is also necessary to go beyond the dichotomous scheme and ask what must happen within the political system when a society experiences the stresses which in the last chapter we identified

[11] Talcott Parsons and Edward A. Shils, *Toward a General Theory of Action* (Cambridge: Harvard University Press, 1951); Talcott Parsons, *The Social System* (Glencoe: The Free Press, 1951).

[12] See, for example, the work of Marion J. Levy, *The Structure of Society* (Princeton: Princeton University Press, 1952); Francis X. Sutton, "Social Theory and Comparative Politics," Social Science Research Council's Committee on Comparative Politics, mimeo.; and Fred W. Riggs, "Agraria and Industria: Toward a Typology of Comparative Administration," in *Toward a Comparative Study of Public Administration*, W. J. Siffin, ed. (Bloomington: Indiana University Press, 1957) pp. 23-116; Robert N. Bellah, *Tokugawa Religion* (Glencoe: The Free Press, 1957).

with the political modernization syndrome. What happens to a society when there is a broad demand for equality and participation, when there is a need for increased capacity or governmental capabilities, and when the processes of differentiation and specialization tend to become more acute?

Some members of the Committee on Comparative Politics of the Social Science Research Council have suggested that it may be useful to conceptualize the processes of political development as involving essentially six crises that may be met in different sequences but all of which must be successfully dealt with for a society to become a modern nation-state.[13]

The Identity Crisis. The first and most fundamental crisis is that of achieving a common sense of identity. The people in a new state must come to recognize their national territory as being their true homeland, and they must feel as individuals that their own personal identities are in part defined by their identification with their territorially delimited country. In most of the new states traditional forms of identity ranging from tribe or caste to ethnic and linguistic groups compete with the sense of larger national identity.

The identity crisis also involves the resolution of the problem of traditional heritage and modern practices, the dilemma of parochial sentiments and cosmopolitan practices, which we have emphasized. As long as people feel pulled between two worlds and without roots in any society they cannot have the firm sense of identity necessary for building a stable, modern nation-state.

The Legitimacy Crisis. Closely related to the identity crisis is the problem of achieving agreement about the legitimate nature of authority and the proper responsibilities of government. In many new states the crisis of legitimacy is a straightforward constitutional problem: What should be the

13 The following analysis of the "crises of development" is based on the forthcoming study by Leonard Binder, James S. Coleman, Joseph LaPalombara, Myron Weiner, and Lucian W. Pye, which will be published by the Princeton University Press as the seventh volume of the Series in Political Development sponsored by the Committee on Comparative Politics of the Social Science Research Council.

relationship between central and local authorities? What are the proper limits of the bureaucracy, or of the army, in the nation's political life? Or possibly the conflict is over how much of the colonial structure of government should be preserved in an independent state.

In other new states the question of legitimacy is more diffuse, and it involves sentiments about what should be the underlying spirit of government and the primary goals of national effort. For example, in some Moslem lands there is a deep desire that the state should in some fashion reflect the spirit of Islam. In other societies the issue of legitimacy involves questions about how far the governmental authorities should directly push economic development as compared with other possible goals. Above all, in transitional societies there can be a deep crisis of authority because all attempts at ruling are challenged by different people for different reasons, and no leaders are able to gain a full command of legitimate authority.

The Penetration Crisis. The critical problems of administration in the new states give rise to the penetration crisis, which involves the problems of government in reaching down into the society and effecting basic policies. As we have noted, in traditional societies government had limited demands to make on the society, and in most transitional systems the governments are far more ambitious. This is particularly true if the rulers seek to accelerate the pace of economic development and social change. To carry out significant developmental policies a government must be able to reach down to the village level and touch the daily lives of people.

Yet, as we have observed, a dominant characteristic of transitional societies is the gap between the world of the ruling elite and that of the masses of the people who are still oriented toward their parochial ways. The penetration problem is that of building up the effectiveness of the formal institutions by government and of establishing confidence and rapport between rulers and subjects. Initially governments often find it difficult to motivate the population or to change its values and habits in order to bring support to programs of national development. On the other hand, at times the effectiveness of the government in breaking down old patterns of control can unleash widespread demands for a greater influence on governmental policies. When this occurs the result is another crisis, that of participation.

The Participation Crisis. As we noted in seeking to define political development, one dimension of the concept involves an expansion of popular participation. The participation crisis occurs when there is uncertainty over the appropriate rate of expansion and when the influx of new participants creates serious strains on the existing institutions. As new segments of the population are brought into the political process, new interests and new issues begin to arise so that the continuity of the old polity is broken and there is the need to reestablish the entire structure of political relations.

In a sense the participation crisis arises out of the emergence of interest groups and the formation of a party system. The question in many new states is whether the expansion in participation is likely to be effectively organized into specific interest groups or whether the pressures will lead only to mass demands and widespread feelings of anomie. It should also be noted that the appearance of a participation crisis does not necessarily signal pressures for democratic processes. The participation crisis can be organized as in totalitarian states to provide the basis for manipulated mass organizations and demonstrational politics.

Integration Crisis. This crisis covers the problems of relating popular politics to governmental performance, and thus it represents the effective and compatible solution of both the penetration and the participation crises. The problem of integration therefore deals with the extent to which the entire polity is organized as a system of interacting relationships, first among the offices and agencies of government, and then among the various groups and interests seeking to make demands upon the system, and finally in the relationships between officials and articulating citizens.

In many of the transitional systems there may be many different groupings of interests, but they hardly interact with each other, and at best each seeks to make its separate demands upon the government. The government must seek to cope with all these demands simultaneously. Yet at the same time the government itself may not be well integrated. The result is a low level of general performance throughout the political system.

The Distribution Crisis.   The final crisis in the development process involves questions about how governmental powers are to be used to influence the distribution of goods, services, and values throughout the society. Who is to benefit from government, and what should the government be doing to bring greater benefits to different segments of the society?

Much of the stress on economic development and the popularity of socialist slogans in the new states is a reflection of the basic crisis. In some cases governments seek to meet the problem by directly intervening in the distribution of wealth; in other cases the approach is to strengthen the opportunities and potentialities of the disadvantaged groups.

The Sequences of Development.   The particular pattern of development in any country depends largely upon the sequence in which these crises arise and the ways in which they are resolved. It is noteworthy that in the history of England, the model of modern democracies, development tended to follow a path in which the crises arose somewhat separately and largely according to the order in which we have just outlined them. The English developed a sense of national identity early, the issue of the legitimacy of the monarchy and government was well established before the problem of expanding participation appeared and, finally, serious issues of distribution did not arise until after the political system was relatively well integrated.

In contrast, development of the continental European system followed more chaotic patterns. In Italy and Germany the prelude of nation-building did not involve a resolution of the issue of national identity. In France questions of legitimacy and the realities of inadequate integration have persistently frustrated national performance and intensified the crisis of distribution. It was, indeed, the cumulativeness and simultaneity of the crises on the continent that produced the striking differences between the European and the British systems.

The story in modern Asia and Africa seems to be closer to the continental experience than either the British or American. In most of the new states the crises are all appearing simultaneously, and governments are, for example, striving to use the distribution crisis to resolve the identity problem. The efforts to raise the standards of living in these cases are in large part related to creating feelings of basic loyalty to the nation, and this procedure raises the question of how stable such states can become if their citizens' sense of identity is tied too closely to the effectiveness of particular policies.

The chapters that follow deal in various ways with the interrelationships of all of these problems. Ultimately any useful theory of political development must come to grips with the types of problems we have subsumed under this list of crises.

PART II

Particular Issues in
Political Development

CHAPTER IV

Democracy and Political Development

IN OUR discussion of the many possible concepts of political development we noted that one view associated development with the strengthening of the values and practices basic to democracy. And there are many who have a deep concern for the prospects of the developing countries who cannot help but feel that all else is secondary to the hope that advancement for these peoples will lead to more democratic societies. It must be remembered that even within these countries the inspiration which fired the dreams of independence and nation-building was often a new-found faith in the principles of democracy. Nationalist leaders in debating the righteousness of their cause customarily employed the vocabulary of liberal democracy.

Yet constitutional democracy is a peculiarly Western institution, and few questions relating to contemporary public affairs are more puzzling and more fundamentally disturbing than that of whether Western political forms and ideals are appropriate or even relevant for the new states of Africa and Asia. Is it reasonable to ask impatient new states, anxious to speed up all the processes of economic and social development, to rely upon democratic institutions and procedures? What is the best way of achieving the modernization of old societies? And is there any relationship between modernization and democracy, and between democracy and nation-building? And finally that most fundamental and disturbing question: Is a commitment to liberal democratic values likely to be a major handicap in nation-building? Doesn't the situation call for hardheaded and singleminded leadership?

DEMOCRACY AND THE NEED FOR ECONOMIC GROWTH

It may be useful to begin our discussion of democracy and political development by frankly confronting the basic argument that new states cannot "afford" democracy because they must place a prior value on economic growth. The assumption behind this point of view is that rapid economic development is likely to be retarded by a pluralistic political system. More specifically, the widespread belief is that efficiency in the allocation of resources and the necessary discipline in controlling current consumption in order to create the needed savings are more likely in one-party systems where there is a minimum of competitive politics. Presumably partisan politicians in competing for electoral support will cater to the people and will not demand of them the sacrifices and postponements of gratifications necessary for national development. And this is believed to be particularly likely with an illiterate and inexperienced electorate. This point of view classifies democracy as a luxury which can best be afforded only after the big push for development. This is also the argument which Indians frequently make when picturing themselves as taking on the tremendous task of raising the standards of living under the handicap of democratic methods.

It has been our contention in Chapter I that most transitional societies will realize more effective administration only if they broaden and more explicitly organize the non-bureaucratic components of the political process. We are prepared to recognize that under certain very special and limited conditions there may be some advantages in highly centralized authoritarian methods. For example, after a period of prolonged disruption, or when there are acutely conflicting objectives of development and little consensus as to ultimate goals for the society, there may be advantages in arbitrary decision-making. In general, however, these conditions do not obtain in most transitional societies, and, as we have observed, the fear of many elites about divisive forces often stems from threats to their own monopoly of power and not to the basic unity of the country. On the contrary, it can be argued that at present in most situations rapid economic growth is more likely to be stimulated by a reduction in authoritarian practices and an increase in popular participation in the nation-building process. It should be remembered that the history of most backward societies is that of authoritarian rule.

The argument for a one-party system and for administrative rule tends greatly to oversimplify the problem of economic development by assuming that development hinges largely on a more rational allocation of resources. In any society the political system must cope with a wide range of demands. Even a one-party system must expend energy and resources in dealing with such demands. It is significant, however, most demands do not entail issues about allocation of material resources. Just the process of participation in a pluralistic system can satisfy the search for identity of large numbers of people and thereby reduce the number of demands which might involve economically relevant resources. On the other hand, a one-party system, oriented primarily to economic development, may find that it can take care of demands only by decisions affecting the use of economic resources. Under such conditions many groups within the society may translate their aspirations into economic terms and thus place an excessive strain on the limited resources of the country.

The goal of economic development can often be better realized if the functional requirements of the political system for integration and for adjustment are met by participation in competitive politics. When the gratification of the goals of economic development becomes also the prime means for realizing the functions of integration and adaptation, the result is likely to be a less efficient approach to the objective of development.

It is of course a part of the democratic ethos to believe that somehow the democratic method is less efficient than authoritarian means. For example, during the last World War the democracies constantly labored under what proved to be a gross illusion that the totalitarian states were more efficient in war-making. Similarly, we have been inclined to suspect that the communists must have some inherent advantages in the cold war. At present the strong drift away from democratic practices in many new countries is frequently justified on the grounds of the supposed greater effectiveness of authoritarian forms in speeding economic development.

No useful purpose is served in minimizing the very great difficulties which confront the transitional societies in their efforts to modernize. It is, however, unfortunate that, confronted with such tremendous tasks, there has been a tendency to confuse standards and to live with illusions. To a disturbing degree the strange idea has been spread within many transitional societies that democracy is linked with inefficiency, muddled actions, and corrupt practices, while authoritarian ways are identified with clear thinking, purposeful action, and firm dedication. Politicians in many such countries have sought to justify all their weaknesses and their lack of standards on the grounds that poor performance records are proof of commitment to democratic methods. The basic point is that competent democratic leadership by inspiring popular participation can, in fact, mobilize greater involvement in the tasks of economic development than is possible with autocratic, but unpopular, leaders.

THE FUNDAMENTAL ISSUE OF INSTABILITY AND ORDER

A second major reason for doubting the validity of democratic values in transitional societies is an appreciation of how weak public order is in many of these states. The contention is that, aside from the inherently optimistic view of the importance of achieving economic development before worrying about the luxuries of democracy, there is the pessimistic prospect that many of these societies may fall into a state of disorder in which all progress will become impossible. In this view the problem of mere political survival must dominate all considerations.

At first blush there is much to this argument, for at the heart of the acculturation process in all transitional societies lies an inherent conflict between the need for order and the need for continuing change.* The diffusion of the world culture is fundamentally disruptive of all traditional forms of social organization. At the same time, however, the process of diffusion demands that societies achieve a new level of order. The state of equilibrium between order and change is thus critical in determining the political condition in any transitional society at any particular moment.

In this context, however, we would note first that the essence of political stability is the ability to realize purposeful change, since stability connotes adaptiveness in the face of changing conditions. In direct contrast, political instability connotes a public policy either too rigid and inflexible to accommodate the changing balance of values in the society or too vacillating and unsure to be able to advance any objectives. Thus political stability can be associated with change that is rationally directed toward satisfying the social needs of the maximum possible proportion of the population, while instability is associated with change that fails to gratify the social demands of the people and leaves an increasing proportion frustrated.

Second, we would note that democratic practices in the new states are often threatened by the mood of frustration so common when there is an excessive gap between aspiration and reality. The dynamic factor in creating such tensions has generally been the uneven and discontinuous process of social change in the direction of greater urbanization, for it seems that in transitional societies the rate of urban growth tends to outstrip the rate of industrial and economic development which is the functional basis of the modern city. People have chosen the life of the city even when they cannot find there the activities usually associated with a modern city, a development which demonstrates that individuals can become acculturated to a modern way of life far more readily than societies can be reorganized.

* The remaining paragraphs in this section first appeared in Lucian W. Pye, "Democracy, Modernization, and Nation Building," in J. Roland Pennock, ed., *Self-government in Modernizing Nations.* © 1964. By permission of Prentice-Hall, Inc., Englewood Cliffs, N.J.

The connection between the general principle of the relationship between political stability and social change and the fact of uneven and discontinuous social change in the transitional societies is demonstrated clearly by the case of the highly trained Asian who finds that he cannot apply his new knowledge and skills in his underdeveloped society. It is similarly demonstrated by the less educated person who has turned to the city in search of a more exciting and richer life and who cannot find activities to which he can hitch his ambitions. It is plain that when institutional development lags behind the pace of individual acculturation the grounds are created for serious personal frustrations.

The great difference between the pace at which individuals can be acculturated to the modern world and that at which societies can be reconstructed is the source of the great human tragedy of the underdeveloped areas. In such circumstances human resources must constantly go to waste or be grossly misapplied. The cycle of ambition and frustration also opens the way to profound insecurities and a subsequent decline in effectiveness and competence. People who have been disappointed too often cannot be effective agents for the great and demanding tasks of nation-building.

When we look beyond the individual we see that most transitional societies lack two of the essential prerequisites for a stable system of representative government. The first is a social mechanism whereby it becomes possible to determine and clarify continuously the pattern of values and interests within the society and relate these to the pattern of power through an aggregating and bargaining process. The second is the availability of appropriate instruments for carrying out public policy once the society has expressed its relative values and interests — that is, an efficient bureaucracy which is not just a domineering power group.

Although the lack of these prerequisites in a transitional society constitutes a basic weakness, it is possible for the society to avoid excessive tensions if those who have political aspirations can be recruited into the elite society and accept its outlook. Indeed, some such form of political tutelage is essential if a traditional society is to adopt a more modern form of political life. The danger always exists, however, that the current elite will strive to maintain its administrative and political monopoly and not permit the development of the autonomous roles of the administrator and the politician. When this occurs, the resulting rise in authoritarianism is reinforced by the fact that the elite is becoming even more isolated from the masses.

The lack of those who can perform the full role of the politician is also a major reason why the gap between aspiration and reality becomes a source of general frustration in many transitional societies. An important but often overlooked function of open and competitive political articulation is that of creating in the minds of the public a better appreciation of the distinction between the plausible and the possible.

In societies experiencing rapid cultural change people are often just beginning to learn that they can change their condition of life through political effort. Since people engrossed in the problems of acculturation tend to stress the forms or styles of behavior, their behavior is guided by their images of an ideal and ultimately desired way of life and not by the realities of the existing situation. They feel that it is no longer appropriate to be restrained by the essentially cautious and shrewd outlook on life common to traditional and peasant societies, but they find it difficult to determine what should be the new and realistic standards for guiding their behavior.

In transitional societies, large, politically significant elements of the population feel that they can expect a new relation to exist between effort and reward but are still unsure what this relation actually is. They tend either to believe in pie-in-the-sky promises or to distrust completely the words of the politician. Hence the role of the articulating and competing politicians becomes important, since it is through exposure to their messages that a public can develop a sense of political realism without losing an appreciation for the appropriate function of idealism. In time the public can learn that in listening to political discourse it is necessary to discriminate between the exaggerated language that constitutes the wrappings of political promises and the actual policy implications that are partially hidden within the messages.

To summarize and to return to our attempt to identify the central cause of political instability in transitional societies, we would point to the lack of an effective relation between the ruling elites and their peoples. We see that in some instances political instability is directly connected with the fact that sudden and sharp changes in intra-elite relations are possible because the key members of the elite do not have any firm commitments to the interests of particular segments of the public and so are free to act according to their personal inter-pretations of what is advantageous in the limited sphere of intra-elite relations. Consequently their behavior often tends to be essentially opportunistic. We see that in other instances the elite may remain united but project to the public only its own views of what is socially and politically desirable. Even though they may believe themselves to be sympathetic to the aspirations of the people they may be in fact isolated in their own world. It is clear that when for any reason the gap be-tween elite and public is excessive there is both opportunity and temptation for any set of would-be leaders, with or with-out valid qualifications, to attempt to fill it — a situation al-most inevitably fatal to hopes for political stability.

DEMOCRACY AND THE FUSION OF THE UNIVERSAL
AND THE PAROCHIAL

We may return now to our original questions about the ap-plicability of Western institutions, and particularly of demo-cratic practices, for the process of nation-building in the new states. It should be apparent from our analysis that we are dealing with a problem that is on the one hand deeply grounded in the context of our particular period of history, but which on the other hand is of such tremendous significance for the development of world history that it does seem to consti-tute a universal problem above all particularistic considera-tions of time and place.

The fundamental problem of nation-building at this stage

of history in most of the new states is that of finding a satisfactory reconciliation between the universalistic dimensions of the world culture and the parochial expressions of the local culture. A modern nation-state represents not only the political applications of all the technologies, attitudes, and knowledge basic to what we have called the world culture but also a unique expression of the local and special interests of a distinctive community of people. The essence of nation-building in the new states is the search for a new sense of collective identity for an entire people — a sense of identity which will be built around a command of all the potentialities inherent in the universal and cosmopolitan culture of the modern world, and a full expression of self-respect for all that is distinctive in one's own heritage.

During the first stages when the world culture is being introduced into a transitional society the process can be greatly facilitated by the application of authoritarian means. Indeed, it is possible to establish much of the infrastructure of a modern state through such imposed methods. Of course colonialism performed this function in many of the new states. Yet the very inadequacies of colonialism as a modernization agent point to the limitations of authoritarian methods in the building of modern states.

More precisely there appear to be three inherent limitations of authoritarian methods in introducing the world culture. First, harsh and apparently unfriendly agents of acculturation may strengthen a people's feeling that the world culture is essentially foreign and hence a threat to the self. The result may be psychological counterreactions and a subsequent rejection of the new imposed patterns. Second, authoritarian methods often increase the tendencies toward fragmentation rather than toward fusion. Acculturation is likely to occur only in limited spheres, and sharp divisions may later appear between those so acculturated and those who have not been so directly acculturated. Finally, authoritarian methods appear to be of value only in creating the role of the administrator and hence of formal government, and not in strengthening the role of the politician and hence of the political process. Consequently, excessively authoritarian methods in first introducing the elements of the world culture can produce a profound imbalance between government and politics, impeding complete nation-building.

At a second stage of nation-building the need is for bringing together the universal and the parochial. This stage requires a more intimate relation between the government and the masses. This is the delicate stage when the particularistic sentiments and the real interests of the people must be brought into the political process without disrupting the requirements of the state apparatus. The merging of the cosmopolitan and the parochial can appear to be done through populist movements and enunciation of nationalist ideologies, but in the main these turn out to be synthetic attempts. For only rarely in human history has it been possible for a creative individual to give expression to the sense of identity of an entire people, and under conditions of rapid social change this is particularly difficult.

The attempts of African leaders to give expression to the "soul of Africa," to find the "African personality," and to identify themselves with the "spirit of Pan-Africanism" reflect this urgent need to bring together the universal and the parochial. Yet often these attempts seem to fail in giving a genuine sense of identity to the emerging polity because what is claimed to be the parochial does not in fact represent specific and concrete interests within the society.

It is at this point that the basic functions of representative government become critical in the nation-building process. If these new societies are going to achieve a new level of integration, they must find methods for giving representation to both cosmopolitan and parochial forces. Out of the interplay of representative politics it is possible for a society to realize a fundamental fusion of elements of the world culture and the indigenous traditions. This is because competitive politics forces people to classify their real interests, to seek a rational relationship between ends and means in their social life, and to distinguish between the realms of private and public policies

— precisely the problem of identity which often plagues people in transitional societies. With competitive politics both individuals and a society can fuse elements of the modern cosmopolitan world with their own historic sense of individuality. This process of blending lies at the heart of the modernization process; and it is this fact which justifies our faith that there is a close association between democratization and modernization.

THE PROBLEM OF INTEREST ARTICULATION AND AGGREGATION

What we have been suggesting is that the concern over the fate of democracy in the new states can be inspired not just by appreciating the basic values of a democratic society but also by understanding the nature of politics as a process by which conflicting interests can be brought out into the open and then adjustments can be made which will maximize the interests of all parties. For this to take place there must be an open process by which interests are articulated and then aggregated into public policies. A basic function of the representative politician is precisely to articulate such interests.

Unfortunately, however, it is often peculiarly difficult in transitional societies for politicians to perform such a role. In most transitional countries the processes of modernization and industrial growth have not as yet proceeded to the stage in which the social structure is sufficiently differentiated and the population adequately specialized to create a wide range of specific interests with quite definite but still limited political objectives. At the early stages of national development the most common groupings still tend to be of a communal nature, with each representing a way of life and a diffuse and unlimited set of interests. Under these conditions specific, concrete political interests tend to appear as either the highly personal demands of individuals or the uncompromising and unnegotiable assertions of distinctive ethnic, religious, or other communal groups.

National leaders in such situations are compelled to speak

to an essentially undifferentiated audience.* Without ready means at hand for measuring the distribution of any specific interests, such leaders may feel that they have no alternative but that of striving to appeal to all by reaching for the broadest common denominator. Hence the propensity to avoid in public discussions the specific treatment of concrete issues and to indulge in emotional and more diffusely nationalistic appeals.

The sum effect of the inadequate processes for articulating particular interests is to weaken the possibilities for a rationally based system of interest aggregation. When leaders are unsure of the distribution of particular interests they cannot follow strategies of systematically calculating the relative appeal of different policies in support of different combinations of very specific concerns. Under such conditions public discussion tends to drift away from the hard realities of social conflicts and to become mired in vague generalities.

This tendency may not have serious consequences for the development of a modern democratic polity if there is open competition among all who might wish to engage in such forms of political articulation. Indeed, the continuous exposure of a citizenry to the exaggerated language, the substanceless promises, and the emotion-tapping appeals of politicians who are avoiding hard realities and disciplined reasoning can produce the widespread sense of skepticism about the potentialities of politics which is a first requirement of a responsible and democratic electorate. Once a people have learned to discount and distrust the pie-in-the-sky language of shallow politicians and to see through the superficial idealism of easy prophets, they have entered the world of modern, sober politics. It is this possibility of immunity through exposure which caused the philosopher T. V. Smith to observe, "They also serve who only articulate."

In most transitional societies the public experience in learn-

---

* The remaining paragraphs in this section are adapted from Lucian W. Pye, ed., *Communications and Political Development* (Princeton: Princeton University Press, 1963), and are being reproduced with the kind permission of the Princeton University Press.

ing to discount the exaggerated language of politics fails to take place because there is little open competition among politicians. Instead of different themes and different combinations of policies competing for public attention, those engaged in political articulation tend to present a common front. Political skill in articulation in such circumstances is not related to sensitivity and artistry in isolating and then aggregating values and issues. Once again the consequence is a propensity to avoid the demands of problem solving in terms of real issues and to stress skill in tapping public emotions. The lack of competition means that for the public the trend is not toward choosing and selecting with a skeptical mind but the more extreme consequence of either becoming completely distrustful and contemptuous of the realm of politics or abandoning any attempt at rational judgment and seeking satisfactions from emotionally identifying with the only ones who speak with power.

The purpose of political articulation is not just the training of a critical and questioning electorate. For transitional societies it might be argued that a more basic purpose of political articulation is that of instilling in people new values and new outlooks. Modernization calls for the transformation of popular tastes and fashions, the creation of novel devices and demands, and the welding together of new loyalties. These are all tasks for the popular politicians, and it might seem that if the politicians all present a common front in articulating the new values, the process of modernization would be facilitated more effectively than if there were conflicting and confusing voices. This is what gives some legitimacy to the charismatic leader, the prophet who would give a people a new sense of direction; and certainly development may at times be greatly assisted by the entire political class of a country all pushing in the same direction and all presenting the same promises for a new future.

The test, however, must be a pragmatic one. For the nationalist leader there is always the danger of failing to achieve the full stature of the charismatic leader and appearing instead as a false prophet. Similarly, if the leaders of a country are united against all aspiring leaders but the country does not seem to be realizing its objectives, it is likely that a sense of demoralization will spread among precisely that class of responsible citizens who are likely to have the critical skills necessary for modernizing the society. When politicians talk about radical programs of change but fail to produce substantive results, the consequence can only be a general debasement of standards throughout the society.

The dilemma of the modernizing politician is that he must strive to bring about in a people a fusion of emotions and skills, a desire for the novel but also a respect for the self. The articulating politician must call both for change according to the ways of the modern and hence foreign world and for loyalty to the sense of historical identity of a people. He must ask people to turn their backs on the ways of their forefathers while still preserving their sense of uniqueness. In many transitional societies he finds it peculiarly difficult to achieve an effective blending because he has so little guidance on what are in fact the real interests of the different groups in the society. What tends to happen is that the articulating politician must generalize his discussion of the parochial and parochialize his treatment of the universal. Unsure of what are the parochial interests in his society, he is driven to creating an idealized and abstracted version of a traditional pattern. At the same time he must present the universal that is at the heart of the modern culture as being merely the values and interests of one apparently parochial segment of the society, albeit this is usually the elite segment. In short, the modernizing politician can easily appear to be cast in the role of wanting to advance only the particular interests of a small elite when he speaks of the goals of modernization, and not being able to understand the values of the specific interests when he talks of the traditional and the unique in his society.

These problems, combined with numerous others, tend to weaken the sense of assurance of political leaders. The very concepts of political representation and of responsible leadership are confused as those with power become anxious about their capability to manage a modern political system. Traditional concerns about status and hierarchy mix with memories of authoritarian administration during the colonial period to produce a need to be assertive and uncompromising in proclaiming personal identity with the national interests.

The sum effect of these various difficulties is confusion over expected standards of performance throughout the society. The process of modernization demands an ever-increasing degree of self-discipline and a widening commitment to the ideals of excellence in all fields of life. The responsibility of the popular politician is to facilitate the transformation of an inchoate political community into a civil society. There is thus a direct link between the ways in which leaders perform the function of political articulation and the possibilities for the emergence of elements throughout the societies which have a sense of competence and which are dedicated to raising the level of society.

STANDARDS OF DEMOCRACY

The question of realistic standards becomes peculiarly difficult with respect to democratic performance because of the almost universal tendency to discuss democracy in ideal, if not idealistic, terms. For most people it is the pureness of democracy which counts, and not so much the practical realities of democratic accommodation to an imperfect world. The tendency to treat democracy in abstract terms greatly complicates the problems of strengthening democratic development in the new states. The difficulty is that leaders are often unsure of what might reasonably constitute democratic behavior in their troubled settings but they are sure they have not achieved the ideals of democracy. Thus they not only often have a deep sense of failure but also may conclude that it is impossible even to aspire to building democratic institutions.

In most transitional societies there is a concreteness about almost all modern political roles except that of the popular politician, who is the critical key to democracy. Colonial administrators provided a flesh-and-blood model of how modern members of a bureaucracy should perform. Asians and Africans have also been exposed to the realities of Westernized judges, magistrates, teachers, technicians, soldiers, and the like.

However, they have not generally had a long history of observing practicing politicians in their own communities. Only in
the Philippines and India has there been a significant history
of men making careers out of politics. In some of the newer
states people have found it necessary to innovate overnight the
role of the politician.

It is true that in many of the countries during the terminal
colonial period there were legislative councils and local, if not
national, elections. These very hesitant steps toward popular
politics may have provided a slight degree of experience with
democracy, but in the main the atmosphere was not one in
which the realities of the politician's role could be vigorously
shaped. The colonial authorities not only were hesitant in
sharing power, but often possessed little understanding of the
practical realities of democratic politics, for most colonial officials entered their overseas careers immediately upon comple-
tion of college and thus had little more than a textbook understanding of democracy in their own countries. These relatively
innocent officials in turn tended to pass on to the Asians and
Africans a textbook version of democracy in the mother country. British officials, for example, often proclaimed that democratic politics should revolve around issues of principles rather
than personalities — as though that was ever the whole story of
British politics. When, subsequently, the Asians or Africans
discovered that they could not conduct their politics without
attaching high importance to personalities they tended to conclude that just possibly they were not fully "prepared" for democracy.

What has been missing in the efforts to instill democracy in
the public life of the new states is a realistic understanding of
what democratic politics actually involves in, say, the compar-
ably unsettled life of the early and rapid urban development
in Europe and America. The story of how American democracy grew and flourished out of the rough and tumble of the
old city machines and of the disciplined ward heelers who inducted generations of immigrant Americans into a public life.
Although Americans at this stage in history may not take great
pride in our Tammany Halls and city bosses, there is no deny-

ing that they did perform useful services which today need to be performed in many of the developing countries where new citizens must somehow be inducted into national politics.

In short, while searching for the proper standards for democratic behavior in the new states it is necessary to look beyond the ideals and to ask what are the tasks that must be performed if there is to be in time a greater growth of democracy. These tasks include not only leadership but the development of citizens who recognize that their relationship to government involves inputs on their side of effort, sacrifice and loyalty, and not just the receiving of services and outputs of governmental policies.

In the light of all these considerations we are led to the conclusion that it will be a slow and difficult process to achieve the substance of democratic life in most of the new states. There is much truth in the often cynically advanced generalization that these societies are "unprepared" for democracy. This is a disturbing conclusion for many people in the West who share a basic sympathy for the struggles of the new states because personally they are committed to the democratic spirit and are naturally inclined to identify with the weak, the poor, and the disadvantaged.

At the same time our analysis suggests a ray of hope for people who do have faith in the powers of democracy, for we have noted that advances in the direction of more democratic practices can produce strength. The advantages do not lie with totalitarian or authoritarian methods. The more political development occurs, the more the advantages of democracy will become apparent. For once people have a greater stake in their society and come to believe that progress is possible, they are more likely to appreciate the rewards of living in more open societies.

The problem of working toward a more open society is above all a test of statecraft. To simply open the door to the ever-wider popular participation in politics of illiterate and insecure citizens can easily destroy any possibility for orderly government. In the developing areas there is a genuine problem of establishing effective administrations and as shown in

later chapters, the threats of insurgency and revolutionary violence are endemic in many transitional societies. There is a
need for firm rule if societies are going to advance toward
definite goals.

The argument in this chapter, as in the rest of this volume,
is that firm rule and efficient administration need not be seen
as the opposite of democratic development, but rather authority and participation must go hand in hand in the building of
modern states. We have sought to stress somewhat the practical
advantage of expanding democratic participation through
strengthening the role of the popular politician because in recent years there has been so much discussion of the presumed
practical liabilities of democracy. It would, however, be unrealistic to carry this argument to the extreme of suggesting
that the problems of popular participation should assume top
priority at all times in the nation-building problem. As the
discussion of the crises of development indicated, we must recognize that matters of administration and governmental rule
which come under the crises of integration, penetration, and
distribution are quite as important in building effective modern states.

Thus, in the last analysis, democratic development involves
more than just the successful dealing with problems of popular
participation. To have democratic government it is necessary
to have government and ordered authority.

CHAPTER V

Personality and Changing Values

IN DISCUSSING the issue of democracy and political development we have stressed the problems of organizing a society, expressing political interests, and carrying out effective public policies. Yet democracy involves far more than these arrangements, for there is also the fundamental question of democratic values and the very spirit of democratic life. Thus the analysis of the potentialities of democracy in the new states must take us into the complex realm of attitude change and personality development. This in turn leads us to the question concerning the character and personality basis not only for democracy but for all modern society. Does there not have to be a fundamental change in the outlook and personalities of people if they are successfully to move from the traditional world into modern life?

Policy-makers and scholars have been equally troubled by how much importance they should place on the role of values and attitudes in the modernization process. Among both groups there have been advocates of the view that the entire process of development depends in the final analysis upon certain changes occurring in the realm of the subjective. According to these, modernization is a state of mind, and a modern political system can be operated effectively only by people who share the lively and rational ingredients of the modern out-

89

look. The task of development thus boils down to the blunt need to change the attitudes and feelings of people.

However reasonable such a point of view may first seem, once it is pushed to its logical extreme even the most ardent champion of the psychological point of view is usually ready to withdraw a bit and acknowledge the independent importance of changes in the objective environment. At this point the voices of those who are more at home with objective phenomena can be heard suggesting that modernization and development revolve around certain clearly measurable changes in the structure and performance of the polity and society. According to this viewpoint the argument about how to best facilitate development is again relatively simple: introduce the essential structural and performance changes — by persuasion if possible, arbitrarily if necessary — and the people will in time make the appropriate changes in attitudes. Evidence can be cited to show that once people have been placed in a developed context they can readily adapt their mind and spirit, and thus there is little need to show excessive concern over such murky matters as the psychic state of affairs of transitional individuals.

Ambivalence, ambiguity, and contradictions with respect to these two points of view can be seen in both the record of colonial administrations and in the thrust of American foreign-aid programs. A striking example of the explicit recognition of the vital importance of subjective attitudes was Macaulay's "Minutes on Education" in 1837. With the British Commission on Indian Education divided equally between those who believed that development in the sub-continent could be most rapidly and effectively advanced by modernizing and strengthening the traditional Indian and Sanskrit culture and those who believed development required the Anglicization of Indian education, Macaulay threw his decisive and unqualified support behind the latter group. In his "Minutes" he rudely stated that all of traditional Indian literature was no match to a five-foot shelf of English writing and that the future of Indian society depended entirely upon the Indian mentality being changed into the model of the educated Western man.

There are countless examples of the opposite view about the importance of attitudes in the history of colonial policies. Indeed, the general assumption guiding administrative rule in most of the British Empire was that development could best be furthered by arbitrarily imposing an administration based on the rule of law and then patiently waiting for the attitudes of the people to come around to an appreciation of such an "enlightened" system of government. Implicit was the notion that all people have the capacity to recognize in time the inherent virtues and advantages of more developed political, social, and economic forms and activities, and therefore the process of modernization requires little in the way of conscious efforts to change people's values and attitudes.

American foreign-aid programs have likewise vacillated between emphasis upon changes in objective conditions to more general efforts to alter attitudes and values. Changing assumptions about the importance of the subjective are to be seen in the swings from technical assistance to capital grants to more inclusive programs of development that were discussed in the first chapter. The case for much of the American foreign-aid effort has rested upon the assertion that direct approaches to improve the conditions of economic life will gradually but effectively alter the opinions and values of people in ways consonant with modern social and political life. In spite of the manifest urgency of the problems of the newly emergent countries, which for understanding people is sufficient justification for maintaining their faith in our aid programs, doubts do constantly creep in that possibly genuine development can never really take place until there has been a prior change in the hearts and minds of the people involved. Hence the new belief, expressed in the Alliance for Progress, that reform may be a necessary precondition for effective aid programs.

The confusion and uncertainty of men of affairs over the place of attitudes in the development process is matched by equal uncertainty and disagreement among social scientists. Difference in emphasis upon psychological and value considerations can be found in the various disciplines concerned with human and social development. In the main, economists have stressed objective considerations and have consequently minimized the significance of the human factor. Many development economists argue, in the tradition of the colonial administrator, that once certain structural changes have been made in the economy and certain capital needs met, then the people — whatever their value disposition may have been — will quickly respond to the common sense of economic logic. To the institution changers it is possible to focus on the objective factors in the situation because they can assume that all men, regardless of cultural differences, have a common capacity for rationality, regardless of whatever else may be tormenting them at the subjective level.

Everett E. Hagen, himself an economist, in a rigorous and penetrating criticism of the leading theorists of economic development, has argued, however, that current economic thinking has failed as yet to provide satisfactory explanations as to how economic growth comes about precisely because of the weakness — and indeed triteness — of the assumptions in these theories about attitudes, values, and motivations, that is, about the non-rational and psycho-cultural dimensions of life.[1]

At the other extreme from the technical economists are those anthropologists who tend to see development almost entirely in terms of changes in deeply internalized values that can only occur with great emotional and psychic stress. Much of the anthropological literature on cultural change emphasizes these difficulties and complexities. There is, however, among the anthropologists a second and somewhat more optimistic approach that suggests effective development can readily take place if there is a happy congruence between particular themes in the traditional culture and the attitudinal requirements of a modern system.[2] Although increasingly in recent years anthro-

[1] Everett E. Hagen, *On the Theory of Social Change* (Homewood, Ill.: Dorsey Press, 1962) chapter 3. Parsons and Smelser make much the same observation about the limits of dynamic economic theory, but in terms of the need to supplement economic analysis with sociological theory. See Talcott Parsons and Neil J. Smelser, *Economy and Society: A Study of the Integration of Economic and Social Theory* (Glencoe: The Free Press, 1956) pp. 246-49.

[2] The writings of Margaret Mead reflect both of these points of view. In

pologists have been making systematic and insightful contributions to our general understanding of change and development, it must be recognized that the traditional thrust of the discipline was in precisely the opposite direction: that of trying to explain how human societies were able to maintain and preserve continuity in their ways of life over the generations. The mystery for most anthropologists was why continuity, rather than how development, occurs.

In recent years social scientists from several disciplines have sought to analyze explicitly the role of psychological considerations in governing the pace and pattern of social, economic, and political development. For example, David C. McClelland has related the different levels of need-Achievement in Turkey and Iran to the different rates of economic growth in the two countries.[3] The unique contribution of McClelland's approach, which calls for the content analysis of children's readers, is that it provides a relatively economical means of measuring aspects of national character differences. Presumably, continued work along the line pioneered by McClelland would provide us in time with substantial objective and measurable data about a variety of peoples that could serve as a solid basis for theorizing about the subjective dimensions of at least economic development.

Another recent effort to expand our understanding of development to include the psychological dimension is the above-

---

New Lives for Old (New York: Will Morrow & Co., 1956) she stresses the extent to which cultural change must involve the effective adaptation of change in a tremendous variety of individual attitudes, feelings, and relationships. In *Cultural Patterns and Technical Change* (Paris: United Nations, 1953) the theme is more in terms of the possible connections between certain traditional attitudes and effective adaptation to change. In the field of political science, David Apter has skillfully presented the second point of view in his comparative analysis of how features of the traditional political cultures of Ghana and Uganda have influenced the different capabilities of the two societies to modernize. See his "The Role of Traditionalism in the Political Modernization of Ghana and Uganda," *World Politics*, XIII, No. 1 (October 1960) 45-68.

[3] David C. McClelland, "National Character and Economic Growth in Turkey and Iran," in Lucian W. Pye, ed., *Communications and Political Development* (Princeton: Princeton University Press, 1963) pp. 152-81.

mentioned study of Everett Hagen, *On the Theory of Social Change*,[4] which utilizes systematically psychoanalytical theories and insights. Hagen relates in a masterful fashion the authoritarian personality configuration with traditional society, and the innovational personality type with developing societies. He then hypothesizes as to the social and historical conditions most conducive to creating family situations that will produce creative personalities. One of the significant contributions of Hagen's work, beyond demonstrating the possible utility of psychoanalytical theory for economic analysis, is that it provides a detailed description in personality terms of the essential characteristics of effective entrepreneurs.

From this very brief survey of the judgment of policy-makers and social scientists about the importance of development of subjective considerations it should be apparent that there is considerable difference not only in interpretations but also in the definition of values and psychological factors. It may therefore help clarify our subsequent discussion to distinguish at this point in our analysis at least three different ways in which people have tended to think about values and attitudes in relation to social and political change.

First, there are those who tend to take the most rationalistic view — they would include most colonial administrators and economic theorists — and who thus see the problems of value and culture change as involving primarily the need to train people to the particular skills and techniques essential to a modern society. This approach to the problem of value change emphasizes precisely those matters most susceptible to the influence of public policy, such as education and formal training. The great advantage in thinking about attitude change in terms of training for skill is seen best in the work of economists concerned with manpower requirements for developing societies. Clearly economic development rests upon the availability of particular mixes of technically skilled personnel, and therefore in projecting ahead the desired pattern of economic development for a particular society it seems to make sense to plan for the training of appropriate numbers of people with the

4 *Op. cit.*

right combination of skills.[5] In the study of political development it would seem possible to engage profitably in a comparable form of analysis that would seek to uncover the range of
political "skills" and attitudes that must be instilled into a
population if it is to produce the kind of citizenry and leadership essential for operating and maintaining a developed polity.[6]

This relatively straightforward and uncomplicated view of
the problem of cultural change as only entailing the learning
of specific "skills" has generally had great attraction to the
leaders of transitional societies, but it has almost invariably
proved to be only a deceptively simple facade for profoundly
complex problems and issues. Time and again traditional societies confronted with the inescapable challenge of the modern
world have responded by proposing that "skill" and "values,"
or "technology" and "culture" are completely separable, and
that the former, being related to "materialistic" considerations, are trivial matters when compared with the latter, which
stands on fundamental "spiritual" concerns affecting the essential identity of the society. Thus it is possible to admit the
Western materialist "superiority," seek to adopt aspects of
modern "technology," and believe that the integrity of the traditional "culture" can still be preserved. As we shall shortly be
observing in some detail, Chinese leaders at the end of the
nineteenth century firmly believed that it would be possible to
preserve their ancient Confucian traditions, in spite of the ac-

[5] For studies that demonstrate such an approach see, for example, *In-
vestment in Education: The Report of the Commission on Post-School Cer-
tificate and Higher Education in Nigeria* (Lagos: Federal Government
Printer, 1960) — customarily referred to as the "Ashby Report" after Sir
Eric Ashby, the Chairman of the Commission. For a discussion of the as-
sumptions inherent in such manpower studies see Clark Kerr, John T.
Dunlop, Frederick H. Harbison, and Charles A. Myers, *Industrialism and
Industrial Man* (Cambridge: Harvard University Press, 1960).

[6] To a very large degree the specific cluster of attitudes and values which
a population must be educated to have if a political system is to be both
modern and democratic is to be found in the pioneering study of Gabriel
A. Almond and Sidney Verba, *The Civic Culture* (Princeton: Princeton
University Press, 1963).

knowledged military superiority of the West, by merely taking over Western "science" and "technology." [7] In the contemporary world we can observe the same argument being advanced by African leaders who feel that there is no disgrace in admitting the need to accept modern technology but feel that they must champion their traditional African cultures and the essential spirit or "personality" of their people.

Unfortunately neither the students of social change nor the leaders of transitional societies have been able to determine precisely the values that must be changed and those that can be preserved if development is to take place. In spite of all the careful work of anthropologists on this subject, we have little solid information. Melville J. Herskovits, for example, with considerable righteous zest, has demolished the two extreme positions of the old-fashioned European who said that African development called for a total change and the complete Europeanization of all life, and the contemporary African leader who calls for an easy return to an earlier "golden age," but in striving to build a more acceptable middle position he could do little better that revert to such fuzzy and almost meaningless generalities as the need in development for adaptations

---

[7] A remarkably articulate debate occurred during the last years of the Ch'ing dynasty among Chinese intellectuals in which the "Reformers" argued precisely that it would be possible to defeat the West by an ingenious adoption of Western science in Chinese schools while still teaching the old values in all other spheres of life. The "Conservatives" on the other hand argued that culture is an interrelated system, that Western science and technology was related to the Judaic-Christian-Greco foundations of Western civilization, and therefore it would be impossible to adopt only Western science without opening the door to all of Western culture. The Conservatives, following the logic of their position, held that even in the face of Western material superiority it was more honorable to preserve the full integrity of Chinese civilization even if this meant an inevitable defeat in time. For studies of this period see S. Y. Teng and John K. Fairbank, *China's Response to the West* (Cambridge: Harvard University Press, 1954); M. E. Cameron, *The Reform Movement in China, 1898-1912* (London: Oxford University Press, 1931); Mary C. Wright, *The Last Stand of Chinese Conservatism* (Stanford: Stanford University Press, 1957); and Joseph R. Levenson, *Confucian China and Its Modern Fate* (Berkeley and Los Angeles: University of California Press, 1958).

and fusion.[8] The great difficulty in any particular situation is that there are no clear guides about how much adaptation is necessary and what form should the fusion take; and as long as these questions cannot be answered on a scientific basis they must inevitably raise profound and explosive feelings among those involved.

We shall have to return to these intense psychological dilemmas, but for the moment we want merely to stress that the apparently straightforward and uncomplicated view of the problem of attitude change as only a need for training in new skills can lead into the very complicated and treacherous realm of psychological tension. As we shall shortly observe, the seemingly easy formula of the distinction between "technology" and "culture" cannot satisfactorily resolve the profound problems of identity which are in fact its origins; but first we must finish our survey of the question of value change and the human factor in social change and development.

A second range of considerations that people often have in mind when discussing the human dimension of development is more directly psychological and involves the motivations, ambitions, and goals of individuals. Modern man and traditional man are clearly moved by different forces and set for themselves quite different goals in their social and personal life. Development thus calls for the instilling of new ambitions and the capacity to be motivated by new stimuli. This is the area of psychological reaction that McClelland and Hagen have focused on in their different ways. There is no questioning the relevance of motivations and ambitions for the developmental process, particularly when attention is centered on economic activities. A modern economy, whether capitalistic or socialistic, calls for people who can find satisfaction in manipulating the material world and in advancing their physical well-being. Indeed, most discussions of the human factor in economic development that go beyond the question of skills come to rest on the subject of motivations; and it is frequently observed that in low-income and traditional societies people are primarily

8 Melville J. Herskovits, *The Human Factor in Changing Africa* (New York: Alfred A. Knopf, 1962) chapter 14.

motivated by religious, cultural, or other non-materialistic considerations, while in developed societies people are motivated by economic considerations of gain and find psychic satisfaction from innovating all manner of development.

Possibly a little less obvious is the relevance of motivations for political development. What ambitions and needs are called for if a people are to achieve an increasing rate of political development? What are the political equivalents of the motivations necessary to inspire economic growth? Within certain crude limits it would seem that imaginative political leadership might call for many of the same psychological characteristics essential to the effective entrepreneur. A high need for achievement and the creative personality can certainly contribute to the making of a forward-looking leadership. In fact, we can think of political development as calling for political entrepreneurs in much the same fashion as economic development depends upon economic entrepreneurs. The need would thus be for leaders capable of energetically seeking to combine people and resources together in order to create new forms of organized activities. Such leaders would have to have certain driving ambitions, combined with a high tolerance for ambiguity; a readiness to innovate, combined with a need to find new forms of order; and ability to channel their aggressiveness to advance their goals, combined with a sensitivity to the desires and needs of those they control.

Yet there are certain difficulties with this analogy with economic entrepreneurship. To begin with, the essential traits for success in the two fields of entrepreneurship can hardly be the same, for history is filled with successful economic entrepreneurs who were dismal failures when they turned their ambitions to the political sphere. Indeed, if we were to take the men and the communities that Hagen has singled out as most nearly representing the ideal types necessary for innovating economic development, we would find that without exception they were peculiarly ineffectual in politics.

Possibly the political entrepreneurship necessary for innovating political development calls for a different combination of psychological traits. In suggesting the need to search for such a trait list, we must immediately add that the task will certainly involve far more than merely shifting from an emphasis upon, say, McClelland's characterization of high need-Achievement to his concept of high need-Power.[9] Even the most traditional political systems provided all the scope necessary for people with high need-Power. Again this is a matter we shall have to return to in a later discussion, and at the moment we can only point to the regrettable fact that although there has been extensive discussion of the personality correlates essential for a democratic citizenry,[10] and also of the individual characteristics of leadership in general, there has been little attention given to the qualities of the innovating leader essential for political development.[11] This is one area that at present holds great promise for rewarding research in comparative politics, particularly because in the last few years an amazing array of striking leaders has emerged in the underdeveloped areas, about whom it is possible to collect extensive biographical data, and who can be readily classified according to their relative degrees of success in bringing about political innovation and development.

Continuing with our discussion of the common confusions about the meaning of the subjective in the area of development analysis, we may note that one characteristic basic to any trait list of effective political entrepreneurs is the capacity for psychic mobility and the ability to mentally place oneself in others' roles, which Daniel Lerner suggests is the hallmark of the modern man.[12] This points to a third area of psychological analysis: the determinants of the capacity of

9 As described in David C. McClelland, *et al., The Achievement Motive* (New York: Appleton-Century-Crofts, 1953); and *The Achieving Society* (Princeton: Van Nostrand, 1961).

10 See, for example, Almond and Verba, *op. cit.,* and Harold Lasswell, *Democratic Character,* published in *The Political Writing of Harold D. Lasswell* (Glencoe: The Free Press, 1951).

11 To some degree Erik H. Erikson touches on this problem, although mainly in terms of the ideological innovator in the religious sphere, in his *Young Man Luther* (New York: W. W. Norton, 1955).

12 Daniel Lerner, *The Passing of Traditional Society* (Glencoe: The Free Press, 1958).

people to relate to each other in effective associational relationships. In our analysis in the next two chapters of both the authoritative and non-authoritative structures and processes we shall be observing at many points that political development is related to an increased ability to organize associations of people and to manage complex structures; and certainly these abilities, both in terms of leadership and membership, depend upon cultural qualities and the psychology of the individuals involved. The process of political development thus involves a shift from the values and sentiments which held people together in traditional political communities and structures to those necessary for more developed ones. This capacity to work together rests upon what we may call associational sentiments and is important in terms of the attitudes and predispositions of both leaders and followers. The art of modern government and politics requires that people work together in ways that will maximize the forcefulness of the collective effort, while preserving the necessary flexibility to give scope for change and innovation.

To a large degree this ability to work effectively together involves what is customarily thought of as a spirit of cooperation; but it also involves much more, including sentiments of trust rather than suspicion, capacity to postpone gratifications and to believe that the benefits for some need not mean damage to others. It is this level of sentiments and values that Edward C. Banfield has so brilliantly analyzed in explaining why the people of southern Italy have such difficulty in improving their material well-being.[13]

In distinguishing between the three levels of skills, motivations, and associational sentiments, we have sought to separate questions about attitudes and values that are frequently mixed when both social scientists and men of affairs think about the human factor in the developmental process. We arrived at these distinctions by looking at the work of those primarily interested in psychology and in economic and social development; therefore the task still remains of translating the rele-

[13] Edward C. Banfield and Laura F. Banfield, *The Moral Basis of a Backward Society* (Glencoe: The Free Press, 1958).

vance of these three levels for the understanding of political development. If we seek to do this, it readily becomes apparent that the question of skills, motivations, and associational sentiments represents another way of defining the central components of the political culture.

That is to say, a political culture is defined in part by the distribution of particular political "skills" and "techniques" among the population as a whole and among the political leadership. At another level the political culture is defined by the motivations that inspire both leaders and followers. This motivational aspect of the political culture governs the spirit in which interests are articulated and aggregated and the intensity with which loyalties and commitments are evoked. The third level of the political culture — that which relates to associational sentiments — encompasses the tone and general spirit of interpersonal relations throughout the political system. It determines the degree to which the leaders are capable of working together and the extent to which the public is ready to be a constructive citizenry.

Before continuing with our examination of the problems of the political culture under the stress of development, we should note that this general discussion clearly suggests that political scientists studying the subjective or human dimension of political development can profitably build upon the work that has already been done on the analogous problem of economic and social development. Indeed, political scientists seeking to probe deeper into the problems of attitude change will certainly have to turn increasingly to the work of psychologists and the specialized students of human character and personality. But in doing so caution is called for. Precisely because there is so much the political scientists can gain from these other disciplines it is particularly important to raise the warning that the psychological problem with respect to political development has significantly different dimensions that are not always treated by the other disciplines.

The political scientist must in the first instance concern himself with the implications of change for both the individual and the society at large, and thus he must strive to relate the

tensions that micro-analysis uncovers with the problems of stability basic to macro-analysis. He must strive to understand the
human factor not alone on its own terms but also as it affects
the performance of a larger system of human relations. The
political scientist may share with the psychologist an interest in
the tensions and conflicts that may arise within the individual
when he is compelled by "circumstances" to alter or reject
some of the props and mainstays of his basic personality that
were deeply internalized during the formative years of his development; but the political scientist must go further and ask
what may be the consequences of these tensions as they cause
individuals to strike back at "circumstances" and thus affect
the environment and the total system.

The political scientist must also treat the human factor
within the context of history; not as a historicist but as an
analyst who recognizes that the vital spirit that fires all effective political communities is an unqualified belief in the
uniqueness and the absolute authenticity of its polity. In ac-
knowledging the place of pride, loyalty, and devotion in the
process of nation-building we must also recognize the positive
role of traditions, of parochial concerns and of primordial
sentiments that are all an ineradicable part of human life.
Others, such as the economists, may be able to focus almost
exclusively on the desirability of maximizing the rational and
the universal, but the political scientist, even in his deep concern for the development of more civil societies must explore
also the legitimate place of the parochial, and of the intensely
emotional and nonrational in human affairs.

In treating the human factor in social change the political
scientist must also give prominence to the universal importance of power in human affairs, and thus of the universal
tendency to ask who is the superior and who the inferior in
political relationships. The anthropologist may content himself with the study of acculturation as though it were merely a
process of one culture rubbing against another; for the political scientist there is the additional massive problem of what are
the consequences of feeling superior and inferior in the giving
and taking of cultural ways. In other fields it may be possible

to think of development as a relatively uncomplicated learning process in which people gradually take on the skills, techniques, and attitudes essential to, say, an industrial society, with possibly feelings of regrets and nostalgia for the simpler ways of the traditional agrarian society of the past. In political development it is impossible to escape from the emotional aspects of power relationships and from the cruel fact that the process of development for most of the world has been linked inexorably with foreign control and domination, with humiliation and weakness, with colonialism.

The psychological dilemma in political development is obvious: to gain respect and dignity in the eyes of the world there must be advances in political development, yet the very content of the specifics of development are inescapably seen as having been the unique attributes of European civilization, of the white man, of those who once humbled and humiliated one's own society. It is precisely the conflict between the need to adopt from others and also to assert the uniqueness, and hence superiority, of one's own culture — the conflict between "technology" and "culture" — that makes us talk about an identity crisis rather than just nationalism. For nationalism is usually taken to imply a joyful and uncomplicated expression of one's indigenous culture.

As much as scholars and objective observers may strive to arrive at concepts of modernization and development which are culture free, the fact remains that for those most in need of political development it is impossible to preserve a firm sense of reality and not acknowledge that historically the critical attributes of development seemed to belong naturally to foreign societies and not one's own tradition. Since politics is a matter of power, and the most basic of power relationships is that of superior and inferior, it is understandable that the problems of political development tend to come the closest to activating sensitive nerves about whether one's society is equal or inferior.

Our intention is not to make too much of this matter of the passions and sensitivities of former colonial peoples. Mature people are to be found throughout the world, and not all remembrances of past associations are negative and emotional. Indeed, for many of the peoples of Asia and Africa it is the most natural thing to follow the manners and practices of, say, British or French or American culture. The point is only that in treating the human factor and the psychological dimension of political development we need to recognize why in transitional societies some matters that may seem to us to represent only simple necessity can be the source of profoundly emotional and seemingly irrational reactions, while other matters that may appear to be gross contradictions and blatant anachronisms can be easily accepted as a part of normal life.

A full appreciation of the subjective dimensions of political development thus requires an understanding of the meaning of change in both the histories of individual life experiences and in the collective experiences of the system as a historical entity. The problem is one of finding the means of effectively translating the rich and subtle insights of individual psychology into the generalized propositions essential for the analysis of systems of aggregate human behavior.

FRAGMENTED POLITICAL CULTURES

The concept of political culture can be of great value in helping the political analyst relate the psychological dimensions of cultural change to the larger issues of political development.[14] Political culture provides a means of linking microanalysis and macro-analysis.

Political culture is the set of attitudes, beliefs, and sentiments that give order and meaning to a political process and that provide the underlying assumptions and rules that govern behavior in the political system. It encompasses both the polit-

[14] The concept of political culture as used in this analysis originated with Gabriel A. Almond. See his "Comparative Political Systems," *Journal of Politics*, Vol. XVIII (1956), and republished in *Political Behavior: A Reader in Theory and Research*, Heinz Eulau, Samuel J. Eldersveld, and Morris Janowitz, eds. (Glencoe: The Free Press, 1956) pp. 34-42. For the development of the concept as applied to ten countries see Lucian W. Pye and Sidney Verba, eds., *Political Culture and Political Development* (Princeton: Princeton University Press, 1965) especially chapters I and XII.

ical ideals and the operating norms of a polity. Political culture is thus the manifestation in aggregate form of the psychological and subjective dimensions of politics. A political culture is the product of both the collective history of a political system and the life histories of the members of that system, and thus it is rooted equally in public events and private experiences. In brief, political culture is to the political system what culture is to the social system.

Stable political systems tend to have relatively homogeneous political cultures within which there is general agreement about the proper limits and functions of politics. In such systems each generation is socialized out of common experience and against a common memory of past traditions.[15] The various agents of political socialization, ranging from the family, the school, and the church to the mass media and the articulations of politicians themselves, tend to reinforce each other or at least appear to belong to the same dialogue about what should be the meaning, the means, and the ends of political actions.

In transitional societies there is great confusion because the political cultures tend to be fragmented and people do not share common orientations toward political action. Without a dominant political culture to guide and shape the various socializing agencies the tendency in such societies is for people to turn to political action not only with quite different expectations but also with socially undisciplined motivations. In all societies people become involved in politics for a variety of reasons, both public and private. The difference is that in more stable systems people must make a greater adjustment of their personal motivations to put them in line with publicly acceptable reasons for political action. Thus in the more established systems it is possible to assume that the private interests of the individual and his personal values are fairly closely related to his public position and to causes he supports. In transitional societies there often is little congruence between public issues and private interests.

15 Herbert H. Hyman, *Political Socialization* (Glencoe: The Free Press, 1959).

Psychologically uprooted people who feel insecure because their old and once highly ordered world has been disrupted may turn anxiously to political action in order to find a new sense of belonging, a new sense of identity. For such people it is not the larger, historical issues of politics and public policy that matter, but what counts is merely the act of participation, of finding new associations. Under these conditions there cannot be a rational linkage between alternative policies and programs on the one hand and the personal preferences and motivations of individuals on the other.

What this means is that the political cultures of transitional societies are not only fragmented but are not deeply rooted in stable psychological orientations of the masses of the people.[16] All the psychological insecurities of people perceiving their primordial communities threatened can suddenly be mobilized for one cause or another, but there may not be deep commitment. The difficulty is that individuals do have profound uncertainties about their individual identities, and at times they may strive to find their identities through identification with large political ideologies. This helps explain the intensity of nationalism and the craving for nationalistic ideologies, such as "Arab socialism," "African personality," "Indonesian socialism," "Islam state," and the like.[17]

But the crises of identity among the individuals also explains the incoherence of such attempts at ideological expression and the faltering of ideological movements that are not

[16] Evidence of such psychological difficulties for various developing countries are to be found for India in Edward Shils, *The Intellectual Between Tradition and Modernity: The Indian Situation,* Comparative Studies in Society and History, Supplement I (The Hague: Mouton, 1961); for Burma in Lucian W. Pye, *Politics, Personality, and Nation Building: Burma's Search for Identity* (New Haven: Yale University Press, 1962); for Mexico in Robert Scott, "Mexico's Political Culture," in Pye and Verba, eds., *op. cit.*

[17] On the intensity and deeper significance of ideology in the developing areas see David E. Apter, "Political Religion in the New Nations," in Clifford Geertz, ed., *Old Societies and New States* (New York: Free Press of Glencoe, 1963); and John H. Kautsky, *Political Change in Underdeveloped Countries: Nationalism and Communism* (New York: John Wiley & Sons, 1962).

built upon highly disciplined organizations. Indeed, once people become associated with disciplined organizations, such as
communist parties, then often ideological search for identity is
replaced by a substantive sense of association that comes from
belonging to a community. This explains the capacity of people to remain firmly committed to communist movements even
when, or especially when, they have little interest in the implications of the formal ideology and policies of communism.[18]

PERSONALITY AND LEADERSHIP

What we have just been saying about the motivations of
mass political behavior in transitional societies is even more
acutely applicable to the behavior of political elites. National
leaders are often quite self-consciously aware that in trying to
give political expression to their own personalities they are trying to define a national identity for their people.[19] A Sukarno
in Indonesia, a Nehru in India, a Nkrumah in Ghana have all
felt that in varying degrees they have embodied the essential
spirit of their culture.

The personality problems of the leadership are, however,
more complicated, for as men who would deal in power they
are likely to be peculiarly sensitive to issues of status, pride,
and self-respect. Feelings of their own inadequacies and awareness of national weaknesses can easily compound each other
and cause the elite to become anxious about the possibilities of
failure. Fear of failure in achieving political development can
lead to high sensitivity to any slights as they desperately
search for dignity.

These general psychological problems that are related to
both the disruptions of traditional societies and the humilia-
tions of past colonial domination tend to complicate the abil-

[18] On the relationship between ideology and organization in communist
movements in transitional societies see Lucian W. Pye, *Guerrilla Communism in Malaya* (Princeton: Princeton University Press, 1956).

[19] On the relationship of the individual personality problems of leaders
to the formulation of ideologies for whole societies see Erik H. Erikson,
Young Man Luther (New York: W. W. Norton, 1958); and Lucian W. Pye,
"Personal Identity and Political Ideology," in *Political Decision Makers,*
Dwaine Marvick, ed. (Glencoe: The Free Press, 1960).

ity of people to perform effectively all the various technical roles essential in building a modern nation.[20] The matter is made worse by the fact that when roles are not well established and fully institutionalized the inevitable conflicts and disagreements of competing interests are likely to be seen as merely the conflict of personalities. Conversely, the clash of personalities cannot be muted by the respectable assumption that differences are only the result of conflicting impersonal interests.

Beneath this problem of the rub of personality and politics in more vaguely structured situations are the deeper psychological problems related to the need to change social values and to react to the demands of what we have called the world culture. It is impossible in a few brief pages to capture all the complex forms of human reactions to the problems of having to incorporate to some degree elements of a foreign culture. We can only very briefly review some of the more typical patterns of reactions that have the greatest effect on the evolving political cultures of the new states.

Newness and Insecurity. At the simplest level there is the very normal reaction of insecurity and uncertainty at confronting new and unfamiliar situations. Much of the psychological distortion of political behavior in some of the new states can be readily attributed to confusion over novelty; and presumably the process of learning will eventually reduce the difficulty if in the meantime the experience of uncertainty does not arouse deeper anxieties.

Newness can also provoke fear and withdrawal, as for example in the reactions of peasants to the attempts of administrators to provide them with new methods and technologies to raise their standard of life. People do find comfort in old and familiar customs, and the argument of efficiency is not always very impressive.

Resistance to the new is a pervasive psychological problem in all attempts at innovation and development in the new states, and it absorbs a great deal of time and effort by all officials who would seek to accelerate the pace of social and economic as well as political development. This is the problem

[20] Hagen, *op. cit.*

that American aid officials and Peace Corps representatives usually have in mind when they speak of the psychological dimensions of the development problem. Unfortunately there are much more profound psychological problems.

Conflicting Values and the Illusion of Being Able to Choose the Best. At a somewhat higher level of self-awareness the problem of "old and new" becomes one of "good and bad" and of who is "best." This is the level at which there has been a great deal of public articulation of the issues of cultural change. Intellectuals in particular have grappled with the problem by discussing such issues as the need to preserve the integrity of traditions and the possibilities of adopting modern technologies to support old cultural values. As we have already noted in this chapter, the dichotomy between "values" and "skills" implied by this division of the "self" and the "foreign" is in fact only a facade for far more complex issues that we shall come to in a moment.

Politically this formulation of the problem has often seemed peculiarly attractive to nationalist leaders, for they can declare that their country is in the fortunate position of being able to choose the best of all possible worlds. They can claim, for example, that they will take the best of the "spiritual East" and the "materialistic West," or that they will preserve the best of traditional, say, African community life while introducing only the best of Western civilization. In practice, however, leaders often find that instead of being on the verge of omnipotence they seem to be slipping into a morass of incompetence; for instead of being able to achieve the golden ideal of mastering the best of both worlds they seem to have the worst. They have neither their romanticized version of the community of traditional life nor the creature comforts of the supposedly materialistic West.[21]

Having led themselves to believe they should be in a fortunate, and indeed uniquely favored, position, they are likely to have profound doubts about their own capacities when they

---

21 For details on the complex anxieties of both administrators and politicians over the possibilities of failure and signs of incompetence see Pye, *Politics, Personality, and Nation Building.*

confront the realities of public life in transitional societies. Thus when the illusion of being able to choose the best of all worlds is shattered, the result can be deeper psychological reactions.

Resentment over Foreign Rule. At this point we come to a deeper level of psychological reactions to the demands of social change and political development involving the resentments people have for once being dominated by Western colonial rulers. There is no question that in the ex-colonial world there are many people who have been grievously damaged by having been treated as inferior beings by arrogant Westerners. It would be relatively easy to collect a long list of examples of thoughtless, rude, if not downright evil-minded, acts on the part of Europeans in the societies they once ruled.

To understand fully the complex psychological reactions in the ex-colonial world it is, however, necessary to recognize that the colonial relationship was one of the most complex and many-sided relationships known to history.[22] And above all, many of the negative psychological after-effects were not related just to evil conduct; under the circumstances even the kindest and most highly inspired acts could produce disturbing consequences. Indeed, it was exactly the capacity of Western culture to try to reach out and help others by sharing dimensions of Western civilization that has produced the profound consequences of colonialism. If colonialism had meant no more than the fact that the strong had mistreated the weak, it would have had no more psychological significance than the routine conquests of history. The central fact of colonialism is that it involved far too complex relationships to be summarized by the simple, unambiguous categories of love and hate, of friend and foe, which are the limits of political confrontation and clash.

The particular patterns of colonialism were extremely varied. Many of them followed a sequence that began with the

[22] Some of the complex aspects of the colonial relationship are explored in O. Mannoni, *Prospero and Caliban: A Study of the Psychology of Colonialism* (New York: Praeger, 1956); John Plamenatz, *On Alien Rule and Self-Government* (London: Longmans, Green, 1960).

positive and comforting relationship of dependency on the part of the weak and the poor toward the strong and the rich. Traditional leaders in Africa, India, and Southeast Asia, for example, took pride and honor in swearing allegiance and fealty to the British monarchy and to British rule. As in all politics, lesser authorities saw nothing disgraceful in accepting higher authorities since they expected the same of those beneath them.

In time, however, the diffusion of the world culture and the changing status of colonial peoples made what had once been acceptable relations into increasingly intolerable ones. As the gap between the outlook of ruler and subject was gradually reduced, the positive feelings of dependency gave way to feelings of the injustice of having any remaining differences. The more the colonial peoples were brought into the modern world, the more they became self-conscious of the issue about being considered inferior.

As the relationship changed and the movement toward independence accelerated, new doubts began to arise. What of the people who had sought to become modern before and who had adopted the ways of their rulers — had they been traitors to their own traditions and to the countries which were now suddenly taking form? This was a particularly haunting question for men who had previously looked forward with enthusiasm and satisfaction to working in the colonial administrations. They had believed they were advancing the interests of their own peoples by excelling in the modern arts of law and public administration. Now with independence what had once been their personal career successes seemed somehow corrupt and questionable. Had they been opportunists, seeking their own advancement over the interests of their community?

Many administrators were able to justify their previous service in colonial administrations on the grounds that they had been competent men of professional skill who had through their abilities advanced the well-being of their societies. The great personal tragedy for many of these men is that the circumstances of public administration in the new conditions of independence often made it appear that they might not be competent. And once they had doubts about their own competence then they could easily have more serious misgivings about whether they might not in fact have been traitors. These doubts were often strengthened by nationalist politicians who were always anxious to suggest that anyone who had worked for the previous regime were turncoats and enemies of the people.

Yet even the most ardent nationalist has problems about the legacy of colonialism. Should a national leader seek to make his society more modern if this means making it more like the West? How can one be wholeheartedly in favor of modern economic development if that means copying the ways of one's former rulers? At the same time, however, most nationalists recognize that they cannot adhere to the outdated traditions of their old societies and at the same time achieve the objective of national dignity in the eyes of the world. Nationalist leaders often have to admit that personally they were profoundly inspired by essentially foreign ideas of, maybe, justice or democracy or national strength. In short, even the most passionate nationalist can have deep feelings of ambivalence about "foreign" and "native" ways. Indeed, as long as the very word "native" seems to have pejorative implications how can an individual be an unqualified nationalist?

These are all problems of personal and community identity. As long as issues of identity becloud the personal lives of people in transitional society there will be uncertainty in the political culture. Gradually, however, as people gain a sense of competence and prove their effectiveness in national tasks these problems will pass away. As new standards are established and men can prove their worth in terms of performance, then the psychological dimensions of politics in the new states will become the same as in any polity.

CHAPTER VI

Law as the Source of Both
Instability and Rigidity

IN OUR initial attempt to gain a sense of historical perspective on the processes of political development we noted that the Europeans who restlessly moved out into the rest of the world constantly felt there was something deficient in societies not governed by an explicit system of law. If we were to focus our attention on the sequence of incidents leading to the establishment of any particular colonial system, we would be able to see readily the extent to which Europeans were driven to make commitments and demands of all kinds because of their notions about the proper place of law in the general scheme of things.

For example, in the nearly three hundred years it took to establish their ultimate administrative empire in Indonesia the Dutch constantly pressed for the creation of a legal order that would be consistent with that they knew in Europe. They were willing to allow traditional forms of authority to remain but steadfastly demanded that such authorities act according to a legal order. When the Dutch East India Company was first established in Java in 1619, it sought to establish a base at Batavia that would permit trading in an environment governed by law. Although in every other respect the environment at Jactra was most inhospitable to enterprise and modernization, once the conditions of law and order were met the physical obstacles of steaming swamplands and rampant malaria did not deter the rapid growth of Batavia, which today as Jakarta is the largest city in Southeast Asia. As the Dutch moved across Java they had to develop working relations with a large array of sultans and local potentates, each with his own tradition of rule and custom of authority. In each locale the Dutch insisted upon the recognition of certain principles of universal law even while supporting parochial, historical forms of rule. By 1830, when Dutch administrative control blanketed all of Java, they had created an extraordinary patchwork of local rulers and direct company-administered areas. The common element throughout this system was the notion that government should be related to law and that administration should be premised upon an explicit legal order.

Relations between the British East India Company and local rulers, first in India and then in Malaya, followed very much the same pattern. Certainly one of the dynamic factors in the clash between Western traders and Chinese mandarins that accompanied the opening of China was this same persistent Western belief that human affairs can be satisfactorily carried out only under a rule of law. If we were to elaborate upon the events which took place in Canton, or the encounters between the British and Chinese which led to the Opium Wars, or the first encounters between Westerners and the Burmese and Siamese kingdoms, we could readily demonstrate this constant ingredient of the West's feelings about law.

LAW, ADMINISTRATION, AND NATION-BUILDING

In tracing the story down through the colonial period to the current era of concern for the development of the newly emergent nations we can observe that these sentiments about law have dominated not just the beginnings of the diffusion of Western culture but the entire history of Western thought about nation-building and political development. The initial Western reaction to the non-Western world was the belief that the essential prerequisite for transforming traditional societies into nation-states was the establishment of codified legal systems. The demand for extraterritorial rights in such countries as China, Japan, and Ottoman Turkey reflected this belief that the critical difference between the modern state and traditional systems of authority was the existence of a universalistic legal system. Presumably, once it was possible to give up the necessity of extraterritoriality in a country, that government could be welcomed into the family of nations as a modern state possessing the full attributes of sovereignty.

Gradually, however, the Westerner learned that in order to change a traditional order into a modern state more than just a legal system was needed. If social and economic intercourse were to be conducted in an orderly fashion, if life was to be made more predictable, and if disputes were to be more effectively managed — that is, if the beneficial effects of a rule of law were to be realized — it would be necessary to supplement legal systems with the powers and authority of rational administration. Law requires order, and a legal system needs the backing of a civil administrative system.

Thus from this insistence that local Asian and African potentates and rulers introduce formal legal processes evolved patterns of indirect rule under which Westerners ought to provide traditional authorities with the benefits of modern bureaucracies. Indeed, throughout the colonial period modernization, progress, and the building of nations was conceived of mostly in terms of the development of two prerequisites — law and administration. Whether champions of the White Man's Burden, hardheaded traders, missionaries, or liberal idealists, all agreed that social and political advancement were substantially wrapped up in the development of law and public administration.

During the colonial period the Western mind made a powerful and enduring commitment to the concept that these two processes or systems are fundamental to nation-building. Gradually the West had to recognize also a political aspect that involved popular participation and the creation of new loyalties to national symbols. In the face of this emerging nationalism the West has, however, preserved the belief that before expression should be given to popular politics a people should have legal and administrative development. The tenacity with which the West has clung to its historic concept of the proper staging of the nation-building process is to be seen in the overriding importance given by American foreign aid to the development of administrative effectiveness in the new countries. Almost no American aid goes to the direct development of political roles or the machinery for popular politics. The overwhelming bulk of our aid is directed to facilitate one or another administratively-supported service or activity.

We have proceeded far enough with this general view of the developmental processes for the moment and must put off any further analysis of the interrelationships among these three elements of the developmental process: law, administration, and popular politics. Let us take instead a more penetrating look at the effects of law on social development during the colonial period.

As we have suggested, the Western mind was groping for a *modus vivendi* to carry on day-to-day relations with what it considered to be exotic and bizarre cultures. The need was for some means of achieving order and predictability in relations that seemed to be dangerously tenuous; instinctively the realm of law seemed to provide a practical solution. Above all, when disputes arose the Westerners felt a desperate need for institutions of mediation and adjudication that could be trusted to adhere to universalistic principles (or at least principles that the European felt to be universalistic according to his cultural bias). Although there were other considerations, such as sentiments about justice and morality, the practical concern about uncertainty and the problem of managing disputes was a fundamental factor in the Westerner's quest to establish his sense of law and order in the non-Western world.

Leaving aside any questions of propriety, it is worth considering whether the West was acting in a rational manner in relating ends to means. Given the goal of conquering uncertainty and minimizing the consequences of disputes, was the introduction of Westernized legal systems an effective instrument? Historically, did the increased establishment of Westernized legal codes and processes in fact reduce uncertainty and disputes in the societies of Asia and Africa?

In any particular country the story was of course exceedingly complex and, as in all massive historical processes, full of many contradictory occurrences. Yet a survey of this period suggests that Westerners were on the wrong track, that their approach tended to intensify the very problems they sought to resolve. It is a commonplace to observe that man in solving one problem often creates many others; but here is one of history's monumental examples of man's determined capacity to stick to a single solution, and the more it was pressed the more it aggravated the very problem it purported to solve.

To put the matter bluntly: the more the Europeans insisted upon Westernized legal systems, the more uncertainty there was in human relations and the more disputes there were which could not be readily managed. In large measure Europeans could cling to their singleminded approach by reassuring themselves that Asians and Africans simply could not grasp the concept of Western law and hence needed more of it over a longer period of time. Their dream was that some day all would harmoniously abide together under a reign of law and order; but in the meantime it was fortunate that the police were a jolly fine lot who seemed to know how to handle troublemakers.

In spite of a widespread belief that Asians and Africans had difficulties in adjusting to Westernized legal systems, we could develop quite a convincing case that in many, if not most, non-Western societies the people responded quite readily to the introduction to Westernized legal concepts and procedures. Indeed, in some cultures the alacrity and enthusiasm of the response was nearly enough to trample under foot the new legal system. For example, when the British East India Company first established a system of courts in Calcutta the exuberance of the Bengali reaction was so great as to make a person wonder if this was not a people with some deep, innate affinity for the legalistic mind and spirit! The romance seems to have continued to this day as the Bengali still seems capable of responding with thrill and delight to the practices of the law. This is not just a subjective judgment, for the facts are that by 1900 one Bengali out of every seventy-four was engaged in some form of litigation.[1] There are few cultures in history that have asked so much of their courts.

The pattern was much the same elsewhere in the colonial world. In Java after the Western impact it appears that the rate of litigation not only kept pace with, but indeed exceeded, the rate of population growth. Economic growth, education, and all the other indices of modernization could not keep up with the rise of Javanese population that in time made the island one of the most densely peopled places in the world. But strangely enough, the rate of litigation did keep pace, with the result that by the end of World War I the island possibly had as dense a rate of litigation as anywhere else in the world.

In Rangoon before World War II, interest in the working of the law took on a sporting quality. Asian business houses customarily set aside each year surplus funds that were invested in energetic searches for profitable lawsuits. Young solicitors were employed to rack their brains and dream up ingenious suits, and older rogues with scheming minds would, for a customary commission, assist in spotting likely targets for such suits.

For another example of the way in which Westernized legal systems produced effects precisely contrary to those intended, we could turn to the area of property rights and the regulation of land titles. One of the prime purposes of introducing codified legal concepts was to ensure greater stability and order in social and economic relations. To the European mind this meant that just as any society had to fall under a single political jurisdiction so each tract of land needed to have its own definite owner. To the European, the prevalent Asian and African practice of not defining precisely who owned what land was bound to create confusion and instability in human relations. Yet a strange thing happened: once colonial governments insisted, for both stability and tax purposes, that clear titles be established for all cultivated lands, extremely stable

[1] Maurice Zinkin, *Asia and the West* (New York: Institute of Pacific Relations, 1953) p. 82.

communities quickly broke down and, instead of continuity and orderliness in the holding of property, land began to change hands in a most chaotic and erratic fashion.

In traditional Burma, for example, families and villages had long worked the land with little sense of precisely who owned it, and with even less feeling that it might be possible to buy and sell real property and to alienate in any sense the ancestral land. Under British rule, however, these same people, once they learned that the holding of land was no more secure than the possession of papers of title, rapidly developed a most casual feeling about having and holding real property. Exposed to the excitingly novel world of buying, selling, and mortgaging property, and more particularly to the prospect that one could fill his pockets with cash by merely putting up the title of family lands as collateral, the Burmese soon lost their old and stable habits and became so impersonally attached to their lands that they readily allowed their plots to change hands two or three times a season in the hopes of making some slight marginal profit. The result was often such a confusion of transactions that the land record officers could hardly keep pace. In short, instead of the law's encouraging predictability and stable relations there was disorderly but extremely vigorous change and transformation.

We could spend much time dwelling on the remarkably lively and darkly ingenious ways in which Asians and Africans have demonstrated their interest in Western law. Unfortunately we must rush right on to the moral of the story, which is that a process and a method that had been introduced to help manage disputes seemed to bring to life such a host of disputes that they soon became unmanageable.[2] In many cases the demands placed upon the courts were impossibly heavy, procedures were consequently often compromised, and in time petty forms of corruption became the only method left for keeping the system together.

2 For an excellent discussion of the way the introduction of Western law encouraged and channelized disputes in India see Jules Cohn, "The Initial British Impact on India: A Case Study of the Benares Region," *Journal of Asian Studies*, XIX (1960) 418-31.

In short, until they were presented with Westernized methods of adjudication, Asian societies had no idea of their potential for disputation. Communities and peoples who had lived side by side for generations suddenly seemed to discover within their relations all kinds of issues calling for legal judgments. This increase in disputes stemmed in part from the tensions produced by the Western impact itself. A variety of social and economic changes — including, of course, the introduction of a Westernized legal system — disrupted the adjustment mechanism in these traditional societies, thus causing the people to become increasingly dependent upon one of the causes of their distress, the novel legal system.

Needless to say, European authorities were perplexed by such developments, and, reasoning that life had probably been more tranquil under the rule of custom, colonial officials began in the first years of this century to press for the revival and inclusion of customary law in the handling of disputes. Probably the Dutch went furthest down this road when, out of a strange mixture of a diffuse and uncontrollable paternalism on the one hand and a rigidly precise and orderly outlook on the other, they compulsively sought to record systematically and make painfully explicit in numerous volumes the extremely subtle and delicate nuances of traditional Indonesian Adat law. Having done very little to make the Indonesians into Westerners, the Dutch amazingly enough were still capable of worrying about whether their charges understood their own traditions. The British were less orderly, less systematic, but the pattern was not too dissimilar in their colonies. The fact that bewigged Englishmen could sit enrobed in a tropical climate and, with all earnestness and patience, seek to explain to natives the essence of their own ancestral or tribal rules must have contributed in some degree to the universal reputation that British culture was singularly lacking in a sense of humor. According to British colonial procedures, officials were expected to respect traditional customs and practices except when they "violated universal canons of reason and propriety." These limits, which were explicitly included in the legal codes of most colonial territories, seem in the main to have been unnecessary, for by the time young British District Officers had finished translating in their own minds the ancient traditions of indigenous cultures they always emerged in a form which was consonant with English logic and English tastes.

If we put aside a fascination with anachronisms and return to our main theme, we observe that European efforts to codify and make explicit traditional legal principles inevitably stimulated disputes by destroying the essential ingredients necessary for handling disputes in most traditional systems. To greatly oversimplify the story, traditional cultures generally depended for the adjudication of disputes upon the wit of the wise and judicious man who, in mediating and in seeking compromise, needed the magic of ambiguous and even contradictory saws and principles. The Western approach of course was to minimize reliance upon the cleverness of individual adjudicators and mediators and to maximize the workings of a standardized and impersonal process of decision-making. The underlying assumption of the Westernized and codified legal system was that all possible problems could be classified according to categories, that the examination of the data would reveal which category was appropriate to the particular case or issue, and that, once category and data were so clarified, a standardized process of reasoning and interpretation would bring anyone versed in the ways of the law to the proper judgment. The illusion here was that all possible categories of problems could be initially defined to prevent the need for any *ex post facto* judgments, and that the data or facts could "speak for themselves" in the sense that once brought to light they would somehow automatically inform all under what category of the law they should be properly classified.

The fallacies in these Western assumptions about the process of adjudication were readily manifest once codified legal systems were introduced into Asian and African societies. Clearly there was always so much room for argument over the interpretation of both data and categories that there could be little certainty about the probable outcome of disputes. At the same time disputes, instead of being snipped out by wise men of authority at any early stage, were channelized by the legal processes and in a sense brought out into the open.

THE ENDURING CONSEQUENCES OF THE INTRODUCTION OF WESTERNIZED LEGAL SYSTEMS

We cannot here go into a detailed analysis of the wide range of social, economic, and political consequences of the introduction of Westernized legal systems into the traditional societies of Asia and Africa. We must, however, note a few of these as we shift our attention from how Westernized law failed in its purpose of reducing uncertainty, managing disputes, and providing stability in social relations during the colonial period to the second part of our analysis, which deals with how, in the post-colonial period when the main interest has been rapid changes, Westernized law has become a major stabilizing factor inhibiting desired development.

The significance of the introduction of Western legal systems is best attested to by the fact that in most Asian and African societies the most important new class to emerge under the colonial system was that of the lawyers. In many colonies the whole concept of education was tied to the aspiration of eventually receiving legal training. And in almost all colonies the law was seen as the queen of professions. There was hardly a great man in those parts of the world who did not either obtain a legal education or aspire to one.

Most critics of colonial practices have felt that the overproduction of lawyers in many of these countries has been a long-run liability for national development. Certainly the existence of large numbers of unemployed lawyers, full of unquenchable ambitions and with time on their hands, free only to nurse their fantasies and to engage in scheming, has not contributed to orderly and stable political life. On the other hand, if there had to be an overproduction of any professional class it may well have been best that it was lawyers, and for two reasons. First, of all the possible ways in which Asians and Africans could have been introduced to the world of explicit and systematic reasoning in relation to empirical fact — which is the essence of Western science and philosophy — the avenue of legal training may have been heuristically the most effective. Second, with respect to the dangers of unemployed intellectuals, it seems that lawyers are the least likely to be destructively radical in their frustrations, for, after all, what is a lawyer without an orderly legal system? As revolutionary in spirit as many Asian and African unemployed lawyers have been, their craving for change has almost always stopped short of anything that might compromise the continuing operation of systems essential for the performance of the profession for which they were trained.

The emergence of lawyers as the new elite in many Asian and African countries meant that the diffusion of political awareness was closely associated with a spreading interest in the workings of the formal law. It would be hard to overstate the many ways in which citizens in these colonial countries became knowledgeable in, and even fascinated with, the workings of the law. Research would undoubtedly reveal that these people have many, very interesting ways of comprehending and understanding the nature of Westernized law.

For our purposes it is important only to note that this approach to understanding government through an acquaintanceship with some legal principles caused a profound confusion over the relationship of form and substance in public affairs. Anxious to impress their colonial subjects with the impersonal nature of justice and the firmness and predictability of Westernized legal systems, the colonial authorities stressed increasingly the majesty of the law and the need for everything relating to the law to be carried out in the proper, prescribed fashion. Asians and Africans learned quickly that even if the slightest error occurred in the procedures it could compromise the integrity of the entire system. A single misplaced comma or an erased word could alter the entire outcome of a case. In the light of this anxious and apparently compulsive concern of Westerners for matters of form and procedure it is not surprising that many Asians and Africans came to believe that the power of the law lay in its rituals. We exaggerate only slightly when we suggest that for significant numbers the almost magical potency of the white man's laws lay entirely in carrying out the right incantations. The sum effect was that in time deference to law became associated with resisting all novel and unprecedented decisions.

Similarly, the colonial experience instilled in many Asians and Africans a belief that the law should be autonomous and subject to the wishes of no man no matter how powerful. Colonial officials constantly argued that they themselves were powerless before the law, and all people were impressed by the fact that corruption occurred whenever the law was bent to the desires of any individual. (Widespread corruption often existed, and in no small measure precisely because of this very attitude about the rigidity of law.) The difficulty was that in the colonial setting there was no formal legislative process that could serve as a balance to the judicial process. With no redress through the possibility of legislative initiation, the people and even the important officials were helpless before the universal requirement of adherence to the impersonal dictates of the law.

The result was that there was no sense of a need to connect the operations of the judiciary with the needs of public policy. The law seemed to have an independent existence, and no one learned how it might be balanced with a legislative process that could open the way to orderly change and innovation.

THE BALANCE BETWEEN LAW, ADMINISTRATION, AND POLITICS

Space does not permit us to elaborate further on how the developing feelings about the ritualistic character and the autonomous nature of the law resulted in those Asians and Africans most committed to their Westernized legal system becoming deterrents to rapid changes in the post-colonial setting. We might be led to draw the conclusion from this analysis that the great irony in these pages of history is that only since the European left the scene have his concepts about the potential influence of the law had their intended effects. Now what was to have been one of the greatest benefits of Western man is often seen as a curse to efficient and vigorous development.

There is a more important lesson to be derived from this

exercise in history. We have been observing that the heart of the problem of change and stability in political societies is the interrelationship between law, administration, and popular participation. During the colonial period we observed the limitations of the legal system in either guiding change or maintaining stability. In the post-colonial era we noted that the efforts to preserve the autonomy of the law put the system out of touch with the popular aspirations of the people in their search for change and development.

Indeed, there is considerable danger that with the rise of popular nationalism in many parts of Asia and Africa the principles of an orderly legal system will become unduly identified with a past and partly-hated period of colonial rule. Thus in time many of these countries may turn against their heritage of Westernized laws. Whenever such extreme reactions do occur, we can expect further setbacks in the process of developing a modern polity. The evidence from the historic process through which Asia and Africa have been traveling suggests that modernization and political development require a delicate but firm and stable balancing of the three aspects of government which we have singled out in this analysis. Law by itself has been inadequate in making modern nations, and even when law has been reinforced by a system of administration, national development has not automatically followed. The development of popular politics, through which a people can give expression to their aspirations and values, is the third essential ingredient of nation-building. However, if popular politics should destroy the other two — law and administration — then in another way the building of a modern polity will be crippled if not destroyed.

The capstone of the process of modernization and political development thus seems to be an inescapable need for leadership that is wise and tolerant but firm, and that, while appreciating the constructive potentialities and respecting the integrity of each of the three ingredients, can also bring the three together in harmonious actions.

CHAPTER VII

Insurgency and the Suppression of Rebellions

THE INEVITABLE disruption of the established social order which is a part of the modernization process tends to weaken all forms of authority in transitional societies. Moreover, people in those societies have conflicting notions about what should be the functions and practices of government, and there is active competition, if not conflict, among the many aspiring leaders who seek to put their ideas into effect and to command the rewards of power. As a result, new governments seeking to express the nationalistic aspirations of their peoples often find they can command little authority.

In this situation it is not surprising that disorder and violence have often been endemic in many of the new states. The problem is further complicated by the great conflict of the era between communism and liberal democracy. Immediately after World War II the communists in nearly all the new states in Asia sought to gain power through armed insurrections. At that time they enunciated the doctrine of "wars of liberation" that in more recent years has become a central feature of the foreign policy of Communist China.

The result has been an increasing problem of insurgency in which new and weak governments have been threatened by determined efforts at terrorism and ruthless violence. The tragic story of Vietnam is the most dramatic example of this problem in political development. As a result of Vietnam as well as incipient insurgency in Africa and Latin America, the United States government during the Kennedy Administration became deeply absorbed with the problems of counter-insurgency. We have sought to develop a doctrine of counter-insurgency policies to match the communist doctrine of "wars of liberation." The problem has been one of trying to create the possibilities of freedom in the face of calculated and diffuse violence.

It would be grossly unrealistic in the face of the vigorous proclamations of the communists to discount the extent to which the enemies of freedom have sought to exploit all possibilities for their so-called "wars of national liberation." Yet it would be equally short-sighted to believe in a simple, "devil" theory and to attribute all civil disorders in the new states to the work of professional revolutionaries. The roots of insurgency lie deep in the social, economic and political confusion that is the state common to transitional societies. In order to gain a full understanding of why the international order has been threatened so extensively by revolutionary wars we must come to an appreciation of all aspects of the fundamental process of contemporary social change so violently disrupting the traditional order in much of the world.

The very process of political development and modernization is inherently revolutionary. Once people are exposed to the modern world they are compelled to see themselves and their governments in a new light. Arrangements once accepted as the normal human condition become intolerable. New hopes arise, new opportunities are perceived, but when change does not bring improvements, the result is more than just widespread restlessness and frustration. There is also a sensed need for action. People want to find new bases of association and new channels for articulating and expressing their search for political identity.

In essence the American response has been one of seeking

ways to eliminate the sources of frustration and dissatisfaction which can be so readily exploited for insurgency purposes. This lies behind many of our efforts at foreign aid. We would not deny that change can bring disruption; we would seek, however, to facilitate change so that the energies released by the transitional process can be turned to constructive efforts. In short, the best defense against irresponsible violence is a constructive and positive view of the entire developmental process. In a sense the concern in this book with every dimension of political development is relevant to the problem of insurgency. The analyses of the problems of developing effective administration, of accepting positively the need for wider political participation, of encouraging the prospects of democratic evolution are all in a very fundamental way important for meeting the problem of civil violence.

Indeed, we must recognize that there are conditions under which the revolutionary spirit of a transitional people reflects an inevitable, and even most desirable, ingredient in the process of effective nation-building. Time and again progress calls for the mobilizing of precisely such a revolutionary spirit, and democracies cannot be built out of a spirit of trying to counter all revolutionary changes.

Ultimately, constructive policies toward facilitating political development must include both vigorous efforts to reduce social and economic disabilities and sincere attempts to build dynamic, and even revolutionary, institutions for political participation. These should be the long-range goals for any constructive policies used to cope with the inevitable disorders of the transitional process. At the same time, however, there is the short-run problem of protecting a transitional society politically and militarily from the calculated attempts of well organized enemies of freedom to use violence to gain totalitarian control of vulnerable societies. The rest of this chapter concentrates on the more limited problem of coping with a calculating enemy. We would stress, however, that the basic problem of insurgency involves all aspects of social, economic, and political development.

ON THE COMMENCEMENT OF REBELLIONS AND THE ART OF CONTROLLING REBELS

In the normal course of events there is little that is easier than looking over the shoulders of those in power and announcing to all the world how they might better manage their affairs.* That is particularly true if the power holders are in distant lands that have strange customs and lack such commonplaces of modern governance as rational and honest bureaucracies, graduated income taxes, political parties that contend over principles in preference to personalities, and economies that can sustain their own growth. In such circumstances the advice can take the ready-made form of suggesting that the governors of such unenlightened societies should, with all deliberate speed, change their peoples over into the image of the liberal, democratic, prosperous, and sober societies of the industrial West.

These disrespectful thoughts about the banalities and moralizations customarily offered as sage advice to the bedeviled governments of underdeveloped countries were provoked by the exasperating difficulty of arriving at any worthwhile principles for guiding governments faced with insurrections. How can one avoid sounding trite when discussing what fragile governments should do when, in moments of extremity, they find themselves besieged by vigorous and irresponsibly ruthless insurgents? Certainly there is no help in telling such a government that it need not have happened if only the ruling group in the threatened state had been more like us. Then what should the advice be?

Our difficulty in confidently providing sound advice on how to deal with rebels is directly related to the inadequacies of our knowledge about the causes of insurrections and rebellions.

Significantly, the problem of coping with armed insurrection has been largely ignored in the modern literature of both military and political science. We must go back to the Renaissance

* This chapter is reprinted with permission of the Free Press, a division of The Macmillan Company, from *Internal War,* edited by Harry Eckstein. Copyrighted © by The Free Press, a Division of the Macmillan Company.

and the early formation of the Western nation-state system to find writers on statecraft who were primarily concerned with the problem of creating republics in the face of insurrectionary attempts by would-be tyrants. This problem was central for Machiavelli; and it is interesting to note that his world was passing through a phase of intellectual and social change similar in many respects to the process of change now taking place in many underdeveloped countries. It does seem that there is a peculiarly close connection between the prevalence of insurgency and the processes of nation-building, and we shall have to examine in a moment why this should be the case. In the meantime it is noteworthy that, once the nation-state became the accepted political unit, Western political thinkers tended to pass over the problem of internal disorders. Hence our continued ignorance about the problem.

Whenever people lack empirically-based knowledge about social and political phenomena, they tend to grope for certainty by turning to moralistic explanations. Once history was largely explained as the consequence of "good" and "bad" kings, and now an equally unsophisticated approach relates insurrections to the existence of "good" or "bad" governments. This moralistic approach is particularly common among Americans, possibly partly because we have had less experience with, and understanding of, insurrections, and partly because of our natural proclivity to moralize about the big events of politics. The Civil War was much too traumatic an experience to have given us an intellectual understanding of the problem of managing threats to civic order. Instead we are inclined to see the problem as one for foreign, and of course less perfect, governments. Indeed, a fundamental article of faith in American political thinking is that any government with a rationally sound administration and morally correct policies will not be threatened with revolts. Also of course the general American sympathy for underdogs and the universal pleasure we derive in seeing any form of authority beset with frustrations have somehow made it seem unsporting to take too serious an interest in devising means for stamping out insurrections.

There is no question that our moralistic approach makes us

deeply uneasy about being in any way identified with governments striving to suppress rebellions. We tend to suspect that any government confronted with a violent challenge to its authority is probably basically at fault and that a significant number of rebels can be mobilized only if a people has been grossly mistreated. Often we are inclined to see insurgency and juvenile delinquency in the same light, and we suspect that, as "there is no such thing as bad boys, only bad parents," so there are no bad people, only evil and corrupt governments. No doubt there is a fundamental connection between the basic American orientation toward the problem of insurgency and our deep-seated belief that good relations between the generations depend primarily upon the parent treating the child with scrupulous fairness and warm understanding. Possibly this belief is the source of our profound anxiety that those in authority can so easily compromise their position by not being precisely just and fair in all their dealings with inferiors.

Although we are not likely to advance far beyond our essentially moralistic understanding of insurgency without the assistance of more scientific knowledge, it may be helpful to observe that other peoples, proceeding also on the basis of relative ignorance, have seen the problem of insurgency in a slightly different light and have relied upon quite different assumptions about the causes of civic disorder.

The British, for example, throughout the colonial era had considerable experience with the problems of controlling rebels, and in the main the British authorities came to adopt the view that most civil disorders sprang from man's inherent and compulsively irrational urge to violence and mischief. If a people is not constantly controlled and restrained by the pressures of society, the dictates of firm government, and the general good sense and instincts of responsibility of men of authority, then it can be expected that there will be an inevitable movement toward disorder and insurgency. Instead of the analogy of bad parents producing delinquent children, the classic British view has paralleled the belief that schoolboys will always misbehave if not controlled by the schoolmaster. It is thus simply the inherent nature of man, in a sense the existence of the id, which is at the root of insurgency. The problem of counter-insurgency is merely that of strengthening social sanctions and developing the superego, which is likely to be particularly weak among less civilized and less technologically advanced peoples.[1]

The classic British view of the causes of insurgency had the effect of making counter-insurgency seem to be normal police work rather than a moral crusade. There need be no feeling of malice toward rebels, and it is indeed truly remarkable how unemotional the British could be in seeking to stamp out civil disorders. Furthermore the fact that a people might turn to violence did not in the classic British view suggest that an insurgency might represent a last resort and a response to an otherwise intolerable situation, as is so natural among Americans. To the British it is quite easy to stir up a people's urge for violence, and therefore little political significance need be attached to the willingness of some people to risk their lives.

In rejecting the moralistic approach, which we have suggested is more common among Americans, the British also tended to discount the possibility that just and fair governmental policy might remove the causes of insurgency. On the contrary, the British have in the main held to the idea that the common run of people have little attraction to or basic appreciation for justice and fair government. It is a moral imperative to rule with justice, but no government should expect to be popular for seeing that fair play is upheld. The traditional British colonial position is that the moral imperative rule of

[1] It is an interesting fact of history that British society overcame a fundamental problem of violence and aggression during the same period that British power was creating peace and order throughout so much of the world. In a very deep psychological sense, British national character seems to have been grappling with the problem of controlling the urge to individual violence just at the time when Englishmen were developing their basic concepts about the causes of civic disorder in colonial lands. For a revealing discussion of the prevalence of violence in eighteenth- and nineteenth-century England and the emergence of British feelings of anxiety over the dangers of not controlling one's emotions, see Geoffrey Gorer, *Exploring English Character: A Study of the Morals and Behavior of the English People* (New York: Criterion Books, 1955).

justice has always created trouble because most subject peoples have little comprehension of justice. This position is of course in direct contrast to the moralistic expectation that fair and enlightened policies can eliminate the very sources of insurgency.

In the strict British colonial view there is, in fact, some question as to whether or not it is appropriate to remove a people's source of discontent even to eliminate the danger of insurgency. For example, at one point when Ghana was still the Gold Coast, local British officials became aware that a frustrated, Western-educated, young lawyer was turning to nationalist agitation because he had been unsuccessful in fulfilling his career ambitions. They requested permission of the colonial office to put aside certain formal regulations in order to give a potential revolutionary a respectable job within the civil service. London denied the request on the grounds that no government has the right to deny men their inalienable right to express personal frustrations with political action.

Traditional Chinese governmental philosophy found the sources of insurgency partly in the moral realm, as do the Americans, and partly in the nature of man's spirit, as do the British, but primarily in the domain of the mind. The Chinese certainly recognized that the immoralities of government and the natural rascality of subjects might, in equal shares, contribute to the downfall of civic order. The basic Chinese suspicion, however, was that insurrections occurred when people got notions in their heads and became confused in their minds. The function of government, for the mandarin, was largely to keep people from endless scheming about life and calculations about how to improve one's lot. Good government should train people to keep to their stations and to accept the structure of society. In the Chinese view the danger of insurgency was closely associated with excessive activity on the part of officials, for, once a government sought to do too much to change the state of affairs, ambitious people were likely to toy with the possibility of further changes. Chinese governmental reasoning, in grossly oversimplified form, held that innovation by government was invariably disruptive and confusing and that confusion about the stability of events was a certain cause for a revolution of rising expectations — which must always in time take on a direct political character. Governments thus invited their own downfalls by opening the eyes of their subjects to too many interesting possibilities of change. Again, here is a view that directly contradicts the assumptions behind the American moralistic approach to the roots of insurgency.

No doubt, all of these approaches contain some elements of truth, for each springs from an appreciation of one of the three basic dimensions of individual personality: man's moral sense or superego, man's spirited energy or id, and man's capacity to reason and to be excited by reasoning — the ego. A deeper understanding of insurgency certainly calls for a much more profound analysis of the relationship between personality, politics, and violence than has been customary. The fundamentally shocking and disturbing character of insurgency has inhibited all societies from serious study of the problem. Americans are not the only ones to have had a traumatic experience. Most colonial governments have been quick to put their experiences out of mind, and thus they have failed to acknowledge and codify their accumulative understanding of how to cope with insurrections. In any case, each outbreak of insurgency seems to call for relearning old lessons, for memories on this subject seem always to be peculiarly short. This propensity of governments to forget as quickly as possible all they may have learned about handling civil violence has been a major factor in inhibiting the development of knowledge and doctrine about insurgency.

There is another reason why a body of Western doctrine on fighting insurrections has not developed, comparable to the principles of war at the international level. The character of any insurrection is largely determined by the peculiar social structure and pattern of political relationships of the society in which it takes place. In contrast, in conventional wars between states that are geographical entities there are more constant factors, like the fundamental character of armies and military establishments, levels of technology, and the more controlled range of situations that can arise when formally organized armies clash on fairly clearly defined fields of battle. The difficulty in generalizing about insurrection arises from the fact that strategies which may be highly successful in one situation may be completely irrelevant in another. As guerrillas must live by their wits, so governments fighting guerrillas must be quick-witted and unencumbered by doctrines.

To some extent the problem created by this diversity of insurrectionary situations can be reduced by thinking in terms of some general categories of insurrections. Brian Crozier, in his survey of the anatomy of rebellion and the art of controlling rebels, employs a classificatory scheme that emphasizes the fundamental realities of postwar international politics.[2] Among anti-colonial insurrections he distinguishes between those directed against British and French rule and between those led by communists and by non-communists. He has a separate category for newly-independent governments combatting either communists or non-communist rebellions. Finally he has a category for non-communist uprisings against communist regimes, which, at the time of his writing, included only the tragic Hungarian uprising and not yet that in Tibet or the 1960 fiasco in Cuba.

For more strictly analytical purposes, particularly if we wish to classify insurrections in greater historical depth, it would probably be useful to establish a more generalized scheme. Such a scheme might be based on three considerations.

First, there is the matter of the organization of the general society in which the insurrection occurs, in particular the extent to which its political and social spheres are integrated. Second, the organizational form of the insurrectionary movement is a major factor that determines the pattern of the struggle. Third, there is the question of the characteristics of the government against which the insurrection is aimed.

Within highly complex industrial societies it is almost impossible for political controversies to develop to the point of sustained and organized violence. In such societies the political issues that may divide the population are less likely to follow

2 *The Rebels: A Study of Post-War Insurrections* (Boston: Beacon Press, 1960).

lines that provide the necessary territorial basis for an insurrectionary movement. The possibility of an insurrectionary movement arising and then employing organized violence depends upon the existence of sharp divisions within the society created by regional, ethnic, linguistic, class, religious, or other communal differences that may provide the necessary social and geographic basis for supporting the movement; and a central authority that is unable to maintain uniform and consistent administrative controls over the entire country. Such situations are most likely to arise in essentially agrarian societies or in countries where there are extreme differences between the pattern of life of the urban and industrialized segment of the population and that of the rural elements.

The relative immunity to insurgency of highly complex industrial societies, at the one extreme, and of homogeneously integrated traditional communities, at the other, points to the crucial reason why the problem of insurgency is so closely related at this time in history to the transitional and underdeveloped new nations of the world. The process of social and psychological disruption that accompanies the downfall of traditional societies opens the way to a host of sharp cleavages within such societies. A general sense of social insecurity may intensify the urge to seek the sense of identity that comes from loyalty to ethnic, regional, or other traditional and parochial associations. At the same time, the process of cultural diffusion, which strikes a society at an uneven rate, can create new divisions between those who are more modernized and those who cling to the old.

The fundamental difficulties of nation-building in transitional societies also appear in the inherent weakness of most central governments. The lack of basic consensus about the appropriate ends and means of governmental action can raise widespread doubts of the legitimacy of the formal government. The bureaucratic ineffectuality of most new governments also raises questions not only about their rights but also about their inherent capacities to rule. The environment is thus often peculiarly ripe for groups to try their hand at creating a new state structure; quasi-states and communities readily begin to arise within the state.

In the context of the second consideration, types of insurrectionary movements can best be distinguished by their goals, their methods of recruitment and indoctrination, their organizational characteristics, and their propensities in decision-making and action. Are the announced objectives of the movement limited goals or total power? What is the relationship between the objectives of the movement and the basis of individual commitment to it? Even though the professed objectives may be of a limited nature, does involvement in the movement carry with it an identification with a total way of life, which can be maintained only by constant seizure of greater power? What are the considerations that guide the decisions of the leaders of the movement? What is their understanding of the workings of politics, and what line of calculations do they follow in conducting the struggle? From such questions as these it is possible to distinguish quite different types of insurrections. Thus, even though the same fundamental social problems may be present in several situations, each particular insurrectionary movement is likely to have its own pattern of development based upon the manner in which discontent is mobilized and given new direction. This basis can be readily seen from the fact that when the communists exploit rural discontent they produce a movement quite different from a traditional peasant revolt. The demands of peasants for justice and a better economic lot can usually be satisfied by means of administrative and legal measures, which have little effect on a communist-organized movement.

In analyzing the character of an insurrectionary movement it is particularly important to distinguish between the propaganda about objectives used by the movement and the actual appeals that attract its membership. Recruitment to violent and revolutionary movements is rarely based on the same considerations that dominate the announced political goals of such movements. This disjointed quality is particularly common in transitional societies, in which people are anxiously seeking a basis for association and personal security at a time when they are not yet prepared to treat political loyalty as a function of rational choice among alternative policies.

The third consideration, the character of the government against which the insurrection is aimed, determines both the range of effective counterpolicies and many of the advantages that the insurrectionary group may exploit. Governments with weak administrative organs cannot carry out many types of fundamental social and economic reform. On the other hand, it should be noted that high administrative standards, particularly with respect to law and order, may intensify and even prolong an insurrection. To a large extent it was true in Malaya, where the British felt it appropriate to mobilize a heavy commitment of resources against an enemy that was at no time able to establish any degree of territorial control. In contrast, the governments of Burma and Indonesia felt it unnecessary to mobilize to the same degree against enemies who maintained territorial bases of operations. This distinction means only that wherever a government is primarily an administrative operation, any threat to law and order is likely to be viewed as intolerable. On the other hand, a government with a more limited definition of its administrative responsibilities is likely to be less sensitive to localized disturbances and to react strongly only to insurgent movements that have developed enough strength to threaten its sovereign powers.

We could greatly increase our understanding of internal wars by isolating the critical considerations or variables under each of these three categories. By relating such variables to each other in terms of systematic hypotheses we could arrive at a typology of insurrections. There is no doubt that the gradual accumulation of empirical knowledge about insurrections must depend upon some such systematic view of the total problem. Only as such studies are carried out can we reduce the webs of myth and fantasy that surround so much of the subject of insurgency.

The problem of understanding the causes of insurgency is not likely, however, to yield readily to such objective analysis because, in the end, the task of understanding causes is far too intimately connected with the task of designing policies to preserve the myth of government legitimacy. Any government faced with a violent challenge to its authority must provide a public interpretation of the causes of insurrection. The hypotheses about the causes of insurgency must not only be plausible, but they must leave the government in an effective position to carry on the struggle. Few governments can accept the view that it was their own policy deficiencies which drove people to violence. Governments more frequently prefer to picture insurrections as caused by misguided people lured on by some false prophet or evil conspiracy. Such a characterization has the virtue of making officials appear to be on the side of reason and their enemies essentially fools. The difficulty with the interpretation, however, is that it usually fails to explain how misguided people can behave with fanaticism.

Once we begin to relate the problem of explaining the causes of insurgency to the problem of governmental decision-making, we come to an extremely difficult area of analysis. In order to illustrate the profound complexities of coping with insurrections, it is appropriate to turn our attention at this point to only a limited aspect of the general problem of insurgency. Specifically, it may be useful to focus on the problems of the decisions that are likely to emerge at the commencement of an insurrection. As a result, we may be able to realize the dual objective of shedding more light on the causes of insurgency and providing some useful guidelines for public policy.

THE INITIATION OF VIOLENCE

The initial decisions of a government confronted with the threat of internal war are usually the most fateful and long-lasting of any it will be called upon to make throughout an insurrection. These decisions tend to have a binding effect, which, to an extreme degree, gives structure and form to the entire ensuing conflict. In a sense the first acts of the government establish the crucial parameters of the conflict because they generally define the issues at stake, the presumed character of the struggle, and the legitimate basis for any eventual termination of the struggle.

The enduring consequence of the initial decisions, both in law and in the administrative and political realms, is one of the important respects in which internal wars differ from international wars. In recent years there has been considerable literature on how slippery war objectives can become in international conflicts. Governments may begin with limited objectives — to repel an invasion, to eliminate a dictatorship — but during the conflict, if all goes well, their sights are usually raised; the goals readily expand to take in total solutions — the reunification of a divided country, or the establishment of a new world order under the United Nations, for example. The dynamics of conflict tend to generate inconstancy of objectives, and the popular response to paying the price for victory is generally a demand for altering the *status quo*.

In contrast, in dealing with insurrections, governments must cling steadfastly to the single objective of maintaining the effectiveness of their claim to legitimacy. Governments cannot admit that their policies prior to the outbreak of violence were incorrect or unjust; even less can they suggest that they have changed their policies in the face of violence and illegal actions. No matter what changes may occur in practice, the formal positions of a government cannot change perceptibly during the course of the conflict. For all the supposed virtues of flexibility in other realms of public policy, it appears that people usually find it hard to associate flexibility with the myths of legitimacy.

This view of the problem is of course that of the government. Rebels, on the other hand, are not bound by the same restraints, and their demands and objectives can therefore easily escalate, as do war aims in international wars, if they seem to be succeeding in the struggle. This difference between the necessarily more rigid position of government and the shifting demands of rebels according to their fortunes is one of the most basic elements of asymmetry in insurrections, an element that does not exist in international conflicts. Indeed, this difference colors all stages of an internal war and dominates all efforts at formal or even tacit negotiations. Governments can usually allow themselves very little elbow room for compromises.

It is customary to overestimate the extent to which insurgents have the initiative in defining the issues at stake and in providing the public with its understanding of the bases of the conflict. In taking the first steps toward introducing violence insurgents can project the first propaganda claims and proclaim their version of the causes of the conflict. In most insurrections, however, the actions and pronouncements of governments are more significant in determining the public's comprehension of the conflict. Government's behavior is usually the test people employ to judge the credibility of insurgents' claims. The government can expect to be judged according to its grasp of reality, its capability of coping with the threat, its chances of controlling the future — in sum, its ability to act as a sovereign authority should in preserving its legitimacy. That is not to say that people readily accept the views and announcements of a government in distress; it is rather to stress that government is conspicuous and that people tend to take their cues from government's own interpretations of its probable effectiveness and its basic capabilities. Rebels claim all manner of injustices; it is the actions of government that add or subtract plausibility to such claims.

One of the first tests of strength between government and rebels is, therefore, to determine who will define the basic issues of the conflict and what should constitute a solution. The manner in which the initial issues are first defined usually becomes increasingly binding and generally determines much of the later strategy that each side follows throughout the conflict. Colonial governments have tended to place very rigorous definitions on such conflicts because colonial authorities have had to demonstrate a monopoly of authority in the colonial societies and to suppress any appearances of an open political process at work. Thus the colonial authorities in most insurrections have posed the problem as one of threats to law and order and of a need to establish security as an absolute objective. This approach was particularly necessary because the main justification of colonial rule frequently was the argument that foreign control provided peace and security in otherwise disorderly societies. Even the lowest level of violence would thus appear as a threat to the legitimacy of colonial rule.

Newly-independent governments have usually tended to adopt far more tolerant standards toward violence within their societies. In part this tolerance arises because new governments have not tended to define the problems of government primarily in terms of administration. On the contrary, the leaders of new governments can see themselves as the political opponents of any potential insurgent group. Their need is only to remain dominant; they do not need to claim the same degree of monopoly of authority that their predecessors in colonial governments had to claim. In some of the new governments in Asia the problem of insurgency has been handled largely by allowing insurgent groups a certain amount of freedom of action so long as they do not become a major challenge to the government. In Burma during the last decade insurgency has become highly institutionalized in many areas, and the same is true in parts of Indonesia.

For both new governments and colonial authorities there is, however, a common problem of defining any conflict for the general public. Governments generally find it difficult to avoid giving a highly legalistic definition to most insurgency conflicts — primarily because one of the basic functions of government is to maintain the structure of the legal system, which is inevitably challenged by any insurgent movement. On the other hand, by characterizing the conflict as essentially a threat to law and order, governments often lose the basis for popular enthusiasm. Governments are expected to provide law and order for their communities, and their publics cannot reasonably be expected to become excited about helping the authorities in their basic tasks. What is more, the failure of a government to meet this basic function is often taken as an indication that the government has failed in other matters. That is one reason why some of the new governments in Asia, when confronted with threats of insurgency, have preferred to define the issue in other than legalistic terms. By accepting the conflict more openly as a political one, a government does not have to admit that the very existence of a conflict has brought its ability to rule into question. The fact that a particular political conflict has led to violence is a reflection only in part upon the ability of a government and can be accepted as a symptom of the weakness of a whole society. In this way a government can reduce its own sense of responsibility for the evolving conflict.

The manner in which a conflict is defined in the beginning is also likely to affect the entire course of an insurrection because it places certain definite limits upon the ways in which an insurrection can terminate. If the government characterizes the struggle as one of maintaining law and order, then it may have no other recourse but to push the conflict to a total solution and to insist that the insurgent organization be completely destroyed and all those who have violated any laws be punished. Thus, in order to convey the sense of seriousness of a budding insurrection, the government may establish objectives that will considerably prolong the conflict. On the other hand, governments that take a somewhat more tolerant view of insurgency are likely to define the conflict in terms that will permit earlier resolutions without forcing the issue to the point of a total solution.

The most fundamental way in which the government can define the conflict is in the way it chooses to characterize individual rebels. Are the rebels to be treated as criminals, and, when apprehended, must they be brought to trial? Or can they be treated as members of an opposing military organization and be handled as prisoners of war? The difference in these two approaches is fundamental and can shape the entire course of an insurrection. If the government is willing to treat those who have opposed it as misguided people who must be brought back into the society, it leaves itself the necessary opening to be able to treat captured insurgents in much the same way as prisoners are treated in international conflicts. If, on the other hand, the government chooses to characterize the conflict as a basic challenge to law and order, it must then treat each rebel as a member of an illegal organization who has committed crimes against the society. A difficult situation often evolves when in the early stages of an insurrection a government tends to take a very stiff view of the treatment of prisoners, while, as the conflict broadens, it may be forced to take a more lenient approach. The British in Malaya, for example, tried very hard at the beginning of the communist-inspired emergency to characterize the struggle as entirely one of criminals challenging the legal order. They then had no alternative but to try all captured rebels. Very soon, however, it became apparent that this approach was impossible if there was to be at the same time any psychological warfare effort to induce people to surrender.

It is always tempting for governments to try to define conflict in terms that will be most meaningful if the enemy should be quickly suppressed. There is the tendency at the earliest stage for a government to characterize the rebels as an extremely minor and even insignificant group of people and to call for the heaviest penalties against those who have perpetrated crimes of violence. The government's need to redefine its conception of the enemy is often one of the first signs that a conflict is moving into a more prolonged and protracted stage.

Decisions in a Relative Vacuum. After emphasizing the crucial significance of the initial decisions in the face of an insurrection we must unhappily now point to the fact that conditions at such a time are generally most inauspicious for making reasonable decisions. As we have suggested, the significance of such decisions is closely related to the long run; yet at the beginning of an internal war the eyes of decision-makers must be more than usually fastened on immediate problems. The crisis of the moment is what impels the government to action, and it is almost impossible for officials to appreciate the extent to which their actions will have full meaning only at a later time.

In part the difficulty lies in the government's tendency to have imperfect information about the intentions and capabilities of insurgent movements. There are the problems of penetrating the rebel movement to ascertain its intentions and of weighing the rebels' capabilities under conditions of open conflict. Can the insurgent leaders hold their following while exposing them to the constant threat of death? What potential do the insurgents have for recruiting replacements? In the insurgents' statements how much is bluff, and how much reflects commitment? As in any politics of challenge and confrontation, rebel leaders' statements must always exaggerate their case and their intentions. The government must therefore ignore almost completely the substance of rebel statements; it must analyze them only for indications of possible strategies. The need to clear up uncertainties is far more pressing than the need to deal with propaganda points.

Government decision-making is further complicated by the issue of whether it is best to over- or underreact to the threat of revolt.

Overreacting occurs when a government decides to mobilize more resources than it believes, on the basis of its most objective analysis of the situation, are necessary to deal with the situation. Underreacting occurs when a government decides not to apply immediately all the resources it believes would be necessary to crush the insurgents in a full test of strength. Governments tend to differ greatly in their standardized modes of reaction to threat and challenge. British colonial procedures have generally followed the pattern of sudden and dramatic overreaction to situations of potential insurrection, and they have tended to introduce countermeasures in quantum jumps rather than by gradually phasing in new policies. By consciously overreacting to the initial challenge — for example, by declaring emergencies, abrogating constitutions, or employing preventive detention — British officials have been able to give themselves room to maneuver and to appear in a generous light if extensive measures turned out not to be actually needed. In direct contrast, the classic Chinese mandarin approach to the threat of rebellion was to underreact and to lie low initially while contriving and baiting various traps that might entice the rebels to show their hands prematurely. Within the margins of these different strategies there is still, however, a basic limit to over- and underreacting, which, if exceeded in either direction, will seriously — and possibly permanently — affect the government's claim to sovereignty and to legitimacy. The hope of gaining room for subsequent maneuvers by overreacting can easily be more than negated if the population reacts to these policies by assuming that the government is panicking and fears that it is losing control of the situation. On the other hand, the policy of underreacting involves the risk of suggesting to the people that the government is naively uninformed about the seriousness of the situation.

In the last analysis, decision-making at the beginning of an insurrection is complicated most by the fact that it must take place in a vacuum, in the sense that officials must accept an entirely new frame of reference for policy before they can appreciate the full facts of the situation. Without having experienced the realities of coping with rebellion, it is almost impossible for officials to visualize the complete significance of looming developments. Even worse, when faced with the prospect of widespread terror and violence, the human imagination is often a peculiarly unreliable guide to rational choice. Government officials in particular are likely to become unsettled when caught in a situation in which they can discern no reliable signposts to responsible and honorable actions. Men who have long been trained to aspire always to the sound and judicious act can become extremely disturbed when suddenly they can no longer determine what constitutes the sound act.

Tension between Innovation and Continuity. This point highlights the basic problem of determining how much innovation in policy is appropriate at the first signs of an insurrection. The instinctive reaction of a government is usually that a drastic situation calls for a drastic response. Every effort should therefore be made to put forward a new and dynamic front. On the other hand, there is the equally compelling need for the government to resist any action that might suggest panic. In deciding on how much change may be appropriate, acknowledgment must also be made of inertia, a powerful force in governmental organizations. Even the best trained and most highly educated governmental bureaucracies can have massive difficulties in trying to adopt new procedures and policies.

Hence the paradox that governments often find, at precisely the time when they are confronted with a radically new development, that they must fall back and rely more than ever upon unimaginative, routine, and essentially commonplace actions. Instead of trying to do too many new things at a time of crisis a government may be better advised to try to do the old things well, for excessive novelty in internal governmental communications can be disastrous when there is equal novelty in developments in the society. That is to say, it is difficult enough for the organizers of government to adapt to a sudden change in their internal structure of organization and procedure. In a moment of crisis it is essential to do the more instinctive thing, and for governments this usually means acting according to what appear to be the dictates of inertia. One of the problems in both Laos and South Vietnam during the last few years has been that government officials have been given so much advice about new and ingenious activities that they have had little time or inclination to concentrate on the elementary and prosaic functions that must be performed as prerequisite to any more elaborate policies.

Responding to Rebel Demands and Propaganda. In internal conflicts there is a powerful temptation for governments to try to refute each and every propaganda point of the rebels. Immature governments in particular tend to be very uneasy about appearing in a bad light, and often officials in such governments are unnerved at the prospect of being described to the world as unjust, evil, and opposed to the flow of history. More experienced governments, and especially colonial ones, usually realize that in the voluminous flow of political verbiage before a crisis of violence very little is likely to stick, for very few people pay much attention to the specific sets of arguments advanced by rebel propagandists. For example, there are probably only a handful of specialists who are now aware of what the Huks, the Malayan Communist Party, or the Indonesian Communists were demanding in their propaganda at the outbreaks of their insurrections.

Inexperienced governments may also be tempted to blunt the vigor of a rebel cause by making concessions to its propaganda. The hope that some yielding will put off the test of strength is not unnatural, but historically it has rarely proved an advantageous maneuver. When, immediately after Burma gained its independence, the Communists began their insurrection, Prime Minister Nu publicly pleaded with the Communists and assured them that his government would accede to all their policy demands. His behavior was understandable; but so was the Western reaction of horror and the Communists' reaction of redoubling their efforts at violence in the prospect of such an easy victory. The price Nu had to pay for learning and for demonstrating to others that the Communist insurgents sought far more than their propaganda objectives indicated was to appear a bit of a fool before his countrymen.

One of the most difficult decisions a government must make is that of judging when the time has been reached when it is no longer possible through any act of public policy to affect the decision of an insurgent group to turn to violence. Almost without exception whenever rebellions occur, governments tend to lag behind events and to hope that it is still possible to divert by means of public policies the trend toward violence. In most circumstances insurgent groups have had to make a firm commitment to employ violence before they have been able to show their strength. Once a revolutionary movement has committed itself to violence, it must carry out a large number of actions affecting its own internal organization, actions that cannot be readily reversed. Once these decisions have been made, the leaders must focus on mobilizing the strength of its membership, and they can be little fazed by developments external to the organization. Any movement that can be bought off at the last moment by changes in government policy probably does not have the sustaining drive and the organizational ability to mount a serious insurrection. The Malayan Communists, for example, made their decision to turn to violence six months before the emergency began, and during that six-month period no government activity shook its determination in the slightest.

Thus when the public first becomes aware of an insurgent movement, certain irrevocable decisions have usually already been made. Outside critics also often become aware of a threatening situation only at a very late stage, and in trying to acquaint themselves with the causes of the insurrection they may assume that social reform policies at an earlier stage might have prevented the conflict. They often fail to appreciate that after a certain point such policies could no longer have altered the situation.

The fact that an insurgent movement makes its firm decisions at an early stage, combined with the fact that a government can never publicly convey all that it knows, creates a peculiar situation at the early stage of any insurrection. During this stage it often appears that each antagonist is following a course of action that is very little affected by the behavior of the other. The issues the government chooses to discuss and the policies it chooses to advance often are irrelevant to the situation of the moment — and at a time when outside critics tend to place the greatest pressure upon the government to carry out policies that may be peculiarly irrelevant at a late hour.

There is thus at a time of crisis a tendency for politics to come to an end and for the possibility of negotiations to all but vanish. This peculiar phenomenon has often encouraged outsiders to think that a modicum of wisdom and sensitivity on the part of either side might have prevented the collision. Once violence has broken out, it is usually easy to argue that a little foresight and a little intelligence could have prevented the conflict. In a sense the collision of government and insurgents is very much like the old story, which George F. Kennan recently repeated, of the two cross-eyed men who bumped into each other on a street in Philadelphia. The first said, "Why in hell don't you look where you're going?" To which the other replied, "Why in hell don't you go where you are looking?" [3]

The Appearance of Ignorance and the Need to Protect Intelligence. Governments are expected to be well informed about all that happens within their sovereignties; the capacity to rule is the capacity to be prepared for all eventualities. But when an insurrection erupts, it often appears to the public that the government must have been ill-informed and unready to cope with the exigencies. More often than not, however, be-

[3] *Russia and the West under Lenin and Stalin* (Boston: Little, Brown, 1960) pp. 10-11.

fore an insurrection breaks out and becomes a social phenomenon, governments are better informed than their critics are likely to credit them with being. Governments often appear to be ignorant of events in part because the problem of dealing with the initial build-up of an insurgent movement and surveillance of rebel activities usually falls within the responsibilities of the police, who are of course notoriously secretive. At this early stage there is usually hope that policing procedures will prove adequate and that there will be no need to cause public concern.

Once violence has erupted, there are other compelling reasons for governments to withhold much of the information they have. As the emerging conflict becomes more sharply defined, it becomes increasingly essential for the government to protect its sources of information and to withhold from the public much of what it knows about developments. The government is thus faced with conflicting demands. It is anxious to convey the sense that it is still master of the situation and fully aware of all developments; but it must be careful not to reveal all that it knows. It must therefore appear at times to have been ill-informed of the developments that it has not been able fully to control. This dilemma often makes a government appear extremely insensitive to reality. In spite of embarrassment to a government, the overriding concern must be the protection of sources of intelligence.

The very essence of counter-insurgency is the collection of intelligence for the government. The advantages guerrillas and terrorists may possess in opposing the far greater resources of the government can largely be countered if the government has adequate intelligence. At later stages in their insurrection whatever advantages of mobility, surprise, and *esprit de corps* the guerrillas possess can usually be more than offset if the government has the crucial intelligence at the right moment. One of the earliest tests of the probable success of the government is its capacity to build up its intelligence and protect its sources of information even at the risk of appearing to be extraordinarily poorly informed.

The Extraordinary and the Ordinary Functions of Government. One of the earliest problems with which a government facing an insurrection must deal is that of determining how much of its energies and activities will be devoted directly to the conflict and what functions will be guided by considerations irrelevant to the conflict. There is a strong temptation at the beginning of any rebellion to attempt to mobilize all the government's powers and to call upon all of its agencies to become engaged in the conflict. There is considerable danger though, if this temptation is followed, that the entire administrative apparatus of government will become politicized and most of its functions perverted.

Stronger and more experienced governments tend to make an early distinction between those resources that will be mobilized for fighting the insurgents and those reserved for normal activities. There is considerable danger of the government's conveying the impression that its entire administrative functions may be acting largely in response to enemy actions rather than according to its own internal impetus. For example, it is a sign of weakness if a government seems to be stepping up its social service functions solely in response to a challenge from the insurgents. The government should be able to convey the impression that it performs many of these functions according to criteria and standards that are not in the slightest affected by the demands of the insurgents.

One of the most difficult problems facing a government in fighting a rebellion is the need to keep separate its ordinary functions and its extraordinary functions. A government has certain basic responsibilities to its society that must be maintained in spite of the threat of insurgency.

This dual responsibility of government to preserve domestic social order while at the same time competing politically with insurgents is very much analogous to the position the United States faces on the international scene when it tries to maintain international order and engages at the same time in competition in the cold war. The genius of government, as well as that of international statecraft, is that of determining the appropriate allocations of effort to these two tasks at any particular moment of the conflict.

CONCLUSION

From these observations about the host of problems that call for decision at the outbreak of violence it is apparent that it is extremely difficult to provide governments with sound and useful advice on how to deal with a threat of insurgency. Our initial observations of the irrelevance of most such advice have been borne out by our subsequent analysis. It is certainly not enough merely to suggest more enlightened and liberal policies of social reform, although such policies clearly have a place in an over-all program of eliminating the threat of insurgency.

Nor is it possible simply to treat the problem of insurgency as essentially identical with that of good and effective government. The dynamics of insurgency have their distinctive qualities. It is only as we gain deeper understanding of how the various aspects of human behavior relate to the causes of insurgency that we can begin to arrive at a sound basis of knowledge for developing policies to cope with the threat of internal wars. In the meantime, however, we can begin to accumulate insights on the art of controlling rebels who would destroy the prospects of democratic development and establish the rule of tyrants.

CHAPTER VIII

Communications and

Political Development

O F ALL the basic functions which underlie the political
process it is appropriate to single out for special treatment the communications function when discussing political development.* For when we speak of the Western impact upon Asia and Africa, of the diffusion of a world culture,
of the reactions of traditional societies to the modern world,
we are in essence talking about the consequences of communications. The shattering of the old social order and the
fumbling attempts to create a new order that will command
respect in the light of cosmopolitan considerations are disciplined events according to the laws of social communications.

There is a peculiarly intimate relationship between the political process and the communications process. For within the
domain of politics the communications process has a fundamental function. Few people can observe at first hand the sequence of acts which constitute even a small segment of the
political process; men must depend instead upon a communications system to provide them with a comprehension of the
substance of politics at any particular time. It is through the

---

* The material in this chapter first appeared in *Communications and
Political Development* (Princeton: 1963), and is reprinted with the kind
permission of the Princeton University Press.

organization of the communications process that the host of random actions representing the pursuit of power by people throughout a society are placed in some form of relationship with each other; that order is established in the sphere of power considerations and a society finds that it has a polity.

The communications process also performs an amplifying function by magnifying some of the actions of individuals to the point that they can be felt throughout the society, in a sense transforming mere "man-sized" acts into "society-sized" acts. To a remarkable degree the difference between private and public affairs is determined by the extent to which acts of individuals are either amplified or ignored by the communications process. Without a network capable of enlarging and magnifying the words and choices of individuals there could be no politics capable of spanning a nation.

Another function of the communications process is to provide the essential basis for rationality in mass politics. A people can sensibly debate their collective actions only if they share a common fund of knowledge and information. And only if they have some minimum appreciation of how others have been informed about the state of affairs can citizens decide upon the wisdom and the validity of the reasoning behind the actions of their leaders.

All forms of political action are based on trying to fathom the unknowable that always shrouds the moves of individuals in a collective context. Thus politics calls for calculations about the nature of others, predictions about the likely behavior of men in different contingencies, and interpretations about the significance of apparently random events. To an important degree the communications process informs the members of a community about the extent to which they can and should legitimately question the motives and intentions of those initiating political actions. The communications process establishes standards which can keep a people from becoming unduly naive or excessively suspicious about what men are likely to do when they have great power at their command. In short, with an effective communications process people can more readily gain a realistic sense of the domain of the relevant in comprehending political motives.

Similarly, the communications process establishes a common framework of considerations as people strive to see into the future. Those who deal in political power are expected to have some of the qualities of the prophet and the soothsayer, for political power always has a dynamic dimension involving the issue of control over future developments. The communications process informs people as to how farsighted or nearsighted their leaders are.[1]

In proceeding along this line of analysis it becomes apparent that the communications process helps a society establish its rules of political causality and define its domain of the plausible. In large part, politics is made up of attributing relationships to all manner of occurrences in a society, and it is the politician who is presumed to be peculiarly sensitive to understanding and interpreting inter-connections among events. In its simplest and crudest form this process involves those in power identifying a connection between their policies and all the good that has befallen the society, and those out of power interpreting all the evil to have followed inexorably from the same policies. The communications process provides a basis for limiting and making explicit the proper scope of political causality so that leaders and citizens can all be compelled to accept the same sense of the plausible. At the same time, by

[1] It is a commonplace to observe that democracies are generally excessively preoccupied with short-run matters of the moment; therefore the question is frequently raised as to whether the democratic process is capable of coping with the long-run problems that lie at the heart of the process of nation-building. It is less commonly recognized that one of the virtues of democracy is precisely that it reduces the time horizon of a people to the limits of sound predictions, and thus it protects a people from the fraudulent claims of omnipotence on the part of pretentious would-be leaders. In a sense a democracy protects itself from insufferable nonsense by treating as political cranks all who make exaggerated claims of seeing further into the future than is possible on the basis of the common, reasoning ability of man. Thus the concern in a democracy for matters which are immediately at hand is in part a reflection of a distrust for all that is falsely clever in the assertions of the prophet, the soothsayer, and the astrologer.

identifying the appropriate rules of responsibility, it can hold the political actors tightly in a web of causality. The communications process thus gives form and structure to the political process by surrounding the politicians on the one side with the constant reminder that political acts have consequences and that people can have insatiable expectations of politics, and on the other side with the warning that illusions of omnipotence are always dangerous even among people who have a casual understanding of causality.

These observations about the relationship between politics and communications have been historically appreciated by those concerned with improving the conditions of government. Indeed, political activists have customarily revealed in countless ways their instinctive sensitivity to the fact that the state of politics is a function of the communications process. Whether the inclination is to control the press or encourage the freedom of the press — a fundamental basis for differentiating among political leaders — without question, all politicians must react to the realities of the communications process. Likewise the citizens of established polities have repeatedly demonstrated their elementary appreciation of the communications process by readily permitting their judgments of its integrity to determine the degree to which they either have faith in, or are cynical about, their political system.

MODELS OF TRADITIONAL, TRANSITIONAL, AND MODERN COMMUNICATIONS SYSTEMS

Much of modernization involves the content of the communication messages flowing through a society. The concerns and ideas which hold the attention of contemporary people are different from those common to traditional communities. With political development must come a broader scope of interest, a greater awareness of human potentialities, a more sensitive appreciation of alternative possibilities of action, and above all a deeper sense of self-awareness.

But aside from the content of communications, development also involves a change in the fundamental structure of the processes of communication. Changes in the institutional basis and the technology of communications go hand in hand with changes in the structure of politics. Therefore, it is useful to distinguish the essential characteristics of the communications systems typical of traditional, modern, and transitional societies.

We would note at the outset that to a large degree there are constant elements in the nature of all communications processes; the universal qualities of both individual man and human society allow for only limited variations. Thus our three categories of society share much in common, and their differences are only relative, not absolute. With this qualification in mind we may begin our comparison by outlining the differences in the structure and organization of the communications system in each of the three types of societies.

The most striking characteristic of the communications process in traditional societies was that it was not organized as a distinct system sharply differentiated from other social processes. Traditional systems lacked professional communicators, and those who participated in the process did so on the basis of their social or political position in the community or merely according to their personal ties of association. Information usually flowed along the lines of the social hierarchy or according to the particularistic patterns of social relations in each community. Thus the process in traditional societies was not independent of either the ordering of social relationships or the content of the communication.

Since the communications process was generally so intimately related to the basic structure of the traditional society, the acts of evaluating, interpreting, and responding to all communications were usually strongly colored by considerations directly related to the status relationships between communicator and recipient. At present among many transitional people there is still a strong tendency to appraise the reliability of various media mainly on the basis of the strength of their personal relationship with the source of information.

A modern communications system involves two stages or levels. The first is that of the highly organized, explicitly structured mass media, and the second is that of the informal opinion leaders who communicate on a face-to-face basis, much as communicators did in traditional systems. The mass media part of the communications process is both industrialized and professionalized, and it is comparatively independent of both the governing and the basic social processes of the country. Both as an industry and as a profession the modern field of communications is self-consciously guided by a distinctive and universalistic set of standards. In particular the mass media system is operated under the assumption that objective and unbiased reporting of events is possible, and that politics can best be viewed from a neutral and non-partisan perspective. Thus, even the partisan press tends to strive to appear to be objective.

A modern communications system involves, however, far more than just the mass media; the complex interrelationships between general and specialized informal opinion leaders, and between attentive and more passive publics, are integral parts of the whole communications system. Indeed, in modern industrial societies, with the ever-increasing ease of mechanical communications and physical travel and the increasingly effective organization of specialization and discipline, there tends to be — paradoxically — an increasing reliance upon direct word-of-mouth communication.[2]

The critical feature of the modern communications system is that orderly relationships exist between the two levels so that the total process of communications has been aptly characterized as involving a "two-step flow." [3] Political communications in particular do not rest solely upon the operations of the mass media; rather, there is a sensitive interaction between pro-

[2] Ithiel de Sola Pool's forthcoming study of acquaintanceship networks confirms the impression that in modern life the world becomes considerably smaller and the individual in any specialized profession sees more of more people in his field than was common in earlier periods.

[3] Elihu Katz and Paul F. Lazarsfeld, *Personal Influence: the Part Played by People in the Flow of Mass Communications* (Glencoe: The Free Press, 1955); Elihu Katz, "The Two-Step Flow of Communications: An Up-to-Date Report on the Hypothesis," *Public Opinion Quarterly*, Vol. XXI (Spring 1957).

fessional communicators and those with influential positions in the networks of personal and face-to-face communications channels. Above all, the interactions between the two levels take the form of establishing "feedback" mechanisms which produce adjustments in the content and the flow of different forms of messages. Those responsible for the mass media are constantly on the alert to discover how their communications are being received and "consumed" by those who control the informal patterns of communications. Similarly, those who give life to the informal patterns are constantly adjusting their actions to ways in which the mass media may be interpreting the temper of "public opinion" at any time.

In short, a modern communications system consists of a fusion of high technology and special, professionalized processes of communications with informal, society-based, and non-specialized processes of person-to-person communications. This suggests to us that the measurement of modernization of the communications system should not be related solely or even primarily to the degree to which a society obtains an advanced technology, mass-media system; instead, the real test of modernization is the extent to which there is effective "feedback" between the mass-media systems and the informal, face-to-face systems. Modernization thus hinges upon the integration of the formal institutions of communications and the social processes of communications to the point that each must respond with sensitivity to the other.

With these considerations in mind let us now characterize in gross terms the essential characteristics of the transitional communications process. Structurally the key consideration is its bifurcated and fragmented nature, for it usually involves in varying degrees one system which is based upon modern technology, is urban-centered, and reaches the more Westernized segments of the population, and also a separate, complex system which conforms in varying degrees to traditional systems in that it depends upon face-to-face relations and tends to follow the patterns of social and communal life. The essential characteristic is that the two levels and separate parts are not closely integrated but each represents a more or less autonomous communications system.

In the transitional society only in an erratic form does the urban-based communications process penetrate into the separate village-based systems. There is usually no systematic pattern of linkage in even a single country, and idiosyncratic considerations are often decisive in determining in any community the individual who plays the role of transmitting and interpreting the communications of the mass media to the participants of the local system. Differences in the particular social and economic status of these transmitters from community to community can have decisive consequences on how the different sub-systems are related to the mass-media system.

In addition to this fundamental division between the urban and the elite level and the village or mass level there is a further fragmentation in terms of the isolated sub-systems. Indeed, in most transitional societies, villages in different parts of the country tend to have less communication with each other than they separately have with the urban centers. The pattern is like the spokes of a wheel all connecting to a hub, but without any outer rim or any direct connections among any of the spokes.

Most of the problems of political development can be thought of in terms of the ways in which such fragmented communications systems can become more effectively integrated into a national system while still preserving the integrity of the informal patterns of human association. Development thus involves the increasingly effective penetration of the mass-media system into all the separate communal dimensions of the nation, while at the same time the informal systems must develop the capacity to interact with the mass-media system, benefiting from the greater flow of communications but also maintaining a sense of community among their participants. The process of development is less dependent upon increased investment in the modernized, urbanized, or mass-media system than it is upon the adjusting of the informal rural systems to each other and to the mass-media system. Indeed, excessive investment in the modern sector may create an even greater imbalance and thus exaggerate more than ever the bifurcated nature of the transitional system as a whole.

Although these structural differences appear to be the critical factors in differentiating the three types of communications systems, we must round out this brief characterization by suggesting some further differences which follow directly from these structural considerations.

There are, for example, certain fundamental differences in the volume, speed, and accuracy with which information is transmitted in the three systems. A modern communications system is capable of transmitting a massive flow of uniform messages to a wide audience. In contrast a traditional system handles only a very limited volume of messages at very uneven rates of speed — some factual news might be spread very rapidly, while more complete information might be disseminated at a much slower pace — and with great variety in repetition.

The sheer volume of communications possible in a mass-media system means that much of the function of the informal, person-to-person level of communications in a modern system centers on screening out specialized information from the mass flow for the consumption of particular audiences. The role of opinion leaders is thus one of investing time and energy in "keeping up" with particular matters and insuring those who are dependent upon them that they are "fully informed" and "up to date" on the special subject. The tremendous volume of communications also means that single messages can easily be lost in the flood, and that the attention of a mass audience can be guaranteed only by repetition.

In a traditional system the prime problem besetting the active participant in the communications process was generally the inadequate volume of information to provide a complete picture. People turned to opinion leaders to learn what could be made out of the limited scraps of information received in the community. The skill of opinion leaders was not one of sorting out specialized information but of piecing together clues and elaborating, if not embroidering, upon the scant information shared possibly by all present. Thus the traditional system depended upon the role of the wise man and the imaginative storyteller who needed few words in order to sense truth and who could expand upon the limited flow of messages.

A transitional system, in combining features of both the modern and the traditional, usually does not have the necessary mechanism for controlling and keeping in proportion the volume, speed, and consistency of the flow of communications. The mass-media sector of the communications process of the transitional societies generally relies heavily upon foreign and international systems of communication for the information it disseminates; but there are no ready criteria for selecting what should be retransmitted, and consequently there is a random element as to the relevance and appropriateness of what is communicated. An even more serious problem is the lack of specialized opinion leaders capable of sifting the messages of the mass-media system and drawing attention to matters of special interest to particular audiences. Instead those in key positions in the face-to-face systems usually are more like the activists in the traditional systems, and hence their special skills lie in expanding upon limited information rather than in selecting from a voluminous flow of communication.

This difference in the skills stressed by informal opinion leaders in the modern and in the transitional systems tends to aggravate the consequences of the very unequal speed of communications at the two levels in the latter system. The mass-media sector of the transitional system, with its inadequately staffed and poorly financed organizations, although it greatly exceeds the capacity of the more tradition-bound systems to retransmit their communications, may not be able to keep pace fully with the international flow of communications.

The limited rate at which the sub-systems can reflect accurately the flow of the mass-media system creates one of the most basic tensions common to transitional societies. For it becomes apparent now that these societies do not have just the problem of relating or fusing elements of the international or world culture with parochial practices and sentiments; they must also usually operate with incomplete or inaccurate images of modernity and partly frustrated expressions of the parochial.

THE ROLE OF PROFESSIONAL COMMUNICATORS

The problems of political articulation are not those of the politicians alone. In any society only a small fraction of political communications originates from the political actors themselves, and this proportion tends to decrease with modernization as increasing numbers of participants without power join the communications process. In a fundamental sense modernization involves the emergence of a professional class of communicators.

In outlining the salient characteristics of the three types of communications structures we observed that in the traditional system there were at best only a very few specialized communicators. The process of communications depended upon people who were performing other social roles. By contrast, the mass-media dimension of the modern communications process not only is comparatively independent of other social and political processes but also constitutes a distinctive industry in both an economic and social sense. Both as an industry and as a profession the modern field of communications tends to generate an ethos and a relatively distinct set of norms for guiding its functions.

There are many qualities of mind and of social class associated with the communications profession. In modern societies journalists, radio and television commentators, and political reporters tend to have a commonly agreed upon standard of excellence by which they can judge each other's performance. There may be much confusion and lack of precision in this concept of profession, but there is one central assumption upon which the entire modern communications industry is built. This is the assumption that objective and unbiased reporting of events is possible and desirable and that the sphere of politics in any society can be best observed from a neutral or non-partisan perspective. Traditional communications processes on the other hand tended in general to be so closely wedded to social and political processes that the very act of receiving and transmitting messages called for some display of agreement and acceptance. Hence in traditional systems the essential structure of the communications process encouraged the expectation that all communications tended to reflect a partisan view, and that there could be no neutral or non-partisan point of view for judging, evaluating, and discussing political events.

The emergence of professionalized communicators is thus related to the development of an objective, analytical, and non-partisan view of politics. As the professional communicators perform their distinctive role as men who understand politics but are not of politics, they are likely to influence their publics to believe that there can be politically neutral institutions at the very heart of public affairs. The evolution of stable, creative politics requires that a citizenry come to believe that in their political system there are certain fundamental institutions which stand apart from immediate partisan conflict, which can be fully trusted and respected, and which can limit but also give meaning to the entire realm of politics. This is to say that there is a direct connection between the integrity of the communications industry and constitutional government.

In transitional systems those who would be the journalists and the reporters of public affairs generally do not have a strong sense of independent professional standards. In large part the economic poverty of the mass media makes it impossible for the society to support a full community of professional communicators. Journalists in most of the new states tend to be so underpaid that they can hardly feel that they represent an independent force capable of criticizing and judging those holding political power. In many of the new countries the journalistic profession has little opportunity for independent development because the most rewarding careers with the mass media tend to be with essentially propaganda agencies for either the government itself or for the dominating political party or movement. Under these conditions writers and communicators may be able to play a constructive role in facilitating the nation-building process, but they cannot assume the lead in training the citizenry to appreciate the virtues and the possibilities of non-partisan, and hence essentially constitutional, institutions.

For these and other reasons the small groups of would-be professional journalists in most of the new countries have a variety of tensions and problems which tend to reduce their effectiveness. On the one hand they are close to all the realities of politics in their countries; they can observe the inner politics of personal relationships so common to transitional systems; they know the seamy side of life and hear all the rumors of corruption; and they are constantly aware of the gap of hypocrisy that always exists in any political system between public pronouncements and inner calculations. On the other hand the journalists tend to be people anxious to become a part of the modern world; they are usually attuned to international developments and the latest fashions and fads in the industrial countries; and above all they tend often to have at least an exaggerated, if not romanticized, view of the performance of modern political systems. Many of these journalists, sensitive to their own difficulties in meeting the professional standards of their counterparts in the more developed societies, become cynical about the performance gap between the politicians in their country and their idealized notions of what leaders should be able to do in a modern society.

The sum effect of these tensions often undermines the ability of the mass media in the new states to educate the citizenry in the basic standards essential for a civil society. The press and radio in such situations are not likely to be inspired to communicate an objective, realistic, and compassionate view of the problems of political life. In recognizing these difficulties of the journalists it is also essential to acknowledge that in a few of the new states some segments of the mass media have heroically overcome the handicaps and have performed truly impressive community and civic services. In recent years there have been many moving examples of isolated newspapers gallantly adhering to the highest ideals of journalistic integrity even when threatened by extreme political reprisals. In other new countries the press has often been the only effective loyal opposition to the domination of a one-party nationalist move-ment. In these countries where the political class has not been able to establish the effective basis of a competitive party sys-tem but in which there has been considerable sympathy for democratic ideals the press has indeed been able to perform a uniquely constructive function by adhering to its professional standards and serving as a temperate critic and oppositional force.

The problems of the emerging journalists in the new states stem not only from the side of the politicians; they are also related to the process of disengagement from the traditions of the writer. In the early stages of modernization, journalists and writers are usually close together, and it is often difficult to distinguish between the two roles. Indeed, in most of the new countries it is customary for the leading authors periodically to perform journalistic tasks and to engage in political reporting and criticism.

Under these conditions the development of a professional journalistic ethos becomes deeply enmeshed in the general problems of the writers' emergence from a traditional role. Viewed from this perspective it becomes readily apparent that the establishment of an objective and politically non-partisan community of specialized communicators is complicated by a host of extremely subtle problems. There is, for example, the tension between the writer's tradition of involvement in life, of commitment to ideas, and of passion for causes and princi-ples and the journalist's standards of detachment and non-partisanship. There are also those problems which the writers and journalists of the new states must share in common: such problems as the relationship of the indigenous languages and the world languages, the difficulties of expressing modern con-cepts in local languages, and the issues about using European languages and the problems of translating world literature into local tongues. Indeed, these problems of the relationship between local languages and the major Western languages represent a peculiarly intense form of the general problem of transitional societies in achieving a satisfactory fusion between the world culture and the indigenous tradition, between the universal and the parochial, a problem which we have already observed to be at the heart of the modernization process.

Leaving aside the problems of the journalist, we should recognize that in the relationship between communications and modernization, writers as creative artists have a vital role. Historically in nearly every case in which a society has experienced a significant movement toward modernization the initiation of the process has been signaled by a literary awakening, by a renaissance in literature. The novel is not only a modern form of communications; it has also been in many transitional societies one of the most effective agents for giving people an understanding of modern life and of new values and new concepts.

COMMUNICATIONS AND CITIZENSHIP TRAINING

Writers and journalists are thus critical teachers in the process of political development. As emerging communicators they are in a favored position to disseminate to others new visions of the realities and potentialities of politics. They clearly occupy a vanguard role in urging people to widen their horizons and to absorb the spirit of the modern world. The diffusion of such new ideas and the stirring of new emotions all have their eventual consequences for politics.

In transitional societies there are usually a variety of diverging and contending notions and sentiments about the nature and the purpose of politics. There are invariably many people of both high and low station in such societies who tend to cling to traditional views and to conceive of politics as primarily designed to provide opportunities for expressing differences in status. Other people may have gained their comprehension of politics during a colonial era, and hence they may continue to expect that government should be a distant, impersonal system of public administration. Still others may have been the children of revolutionary and nationalist movements and have the permanent expectations that politics should be a pure expression of emotion and idealism. Others of the same era may have arrived at a cynical and essentially opportunistic outlook as they have learned to cope with radically changing times. In all transitional societies there are those with mature sentiments and rational outlooks on the functions of government.

The writers and journalists have a unique role in helping the people with all of these different orientations to arrive at working agreements on fundamentals. The building of consensus does not call for a single, common orientation of all toward the state and toward the political realm. On the contrary, pluralism is the very essence of modern society. But pluralism requires that there be a minimum, shared fund of understanding; and it is indeed the unique technological character of the mass media which makes them a preeminent agent for establishing that fund of understanding. By the very act of reaching out to a broad audience with a common message the mass media can instill in people the feeling that they in turn belong to a definable community in which it may not be either necessary or likely for everyone to be in general agreement on all matters. It would seem that the mass media in the new states can be either an instrument of collective indoctrination seeking to replace confusion with one point of view or can become vehicles for community building through which people with different points of view can learn to associate with each other.

The position of the mass media in the new states is more complex than that of being an agent of political socialization, for these modernized components of the communications process are really involved in political re-socialization. That is to say, in seeking to train people to an understanding of the new institutions of the state the mass media must communicate with people who have already reached what they feel to be a mature understanding of politics but is in fact an understanding relevant to a traditional or a colonial world which no longer exists. Hence the mass media are not simply a part of a continuous and coherent training process, as the major socializing agents can be in a stable society, but rather they must be a part of a process of discontinuous change. Thus it is that the mass media, in providing a new basis for understanding politics and for interpreting the realm of government, become involved in the most complex and psychologically intense problems of transitional societies.

Much of recent research on the influences of the mass media on American audiences might bring into question the extent to which the mass media can be reasonably expected to contribute to a quickening understanding of responsible politics among transitional peoples. This research suggests that underlying a population's response to the mass media is a principle of selectivity according to which individuals are likely to expose themselves only to communications that they find to be meaningful and that confirm their predispositions. People are therefore inclined to be responsive only to the familiar and that which matches their interests and their standards of taste. It is this principle of selectivity that apparently limits the educational potentialities of the mass media and therefore casts doubt on the possibility that in the new states the process of consensus building can be rapidly realized by the conscious employment of the media.

There are, however, grounds for questioning whether the principle of selectivity applies, at least to the same degree, in transitional societies as it does in industrial ones. In the West the individual finds himself in an environment that is nearly saturated by the mass media, and he must develop mechanisms for warding off the massive and omnipresent pressures of all the different competing forms of communications. Clearly it is impossible in such societies for a person to expose himself to the overpowering bulk of the communications being disseminated, and therefore, as a means of self-defense, he must develop the capacity to ignore much and to become selective in his responses.

In most of the new states the atmosphere is not saturated with communications; the mass media are novel and can still provoke curiosity. In many Asian and African countries there is only one local radio station or at best two stations that compete for attention; and the volume of newspapers and magazines is so limited that competent readers are usually constantly hungry for more reading matter. Under these conditions of relative sparcity of media it appears that people do not develop the same attitudes of selectivity, and therefore in transitional societies the media can in fact play a far more potent role in political education than in the saturated societies.

In suggesting that a more positive view should be taken of the political socializing capabilities of the mass media in the new states we do not want to minimize the difficulties that still exist. In many of these societies people may be willing and even eager to expose themselves to the media, and they may be fully able to comprehend the messages, but the results still may not be more effective political participation. There is in many transitional societies a need for people to develop a new appreciation of the possible functions of political information and in particular to learn that knowledge can appropriately lead to action. In many traditional systems the mass of the people might be quite well informed about high politics; they might be eager followers of court politics and even appreciate many of the fine points of elite intrigue and maneuver. But it would never occur to the subjects in such societies that their information and knowledge about politics should in any way guide their behavior. They have always been observers, and even if they became connoisseurs they would remain observers. At present there are still in many of the transitional societies large segments of people who should be changing their status from observing subject to participating citizen but who, in spite of being adequately knowledgeable about public affairs, remain immobilized.

Indeed it may often be that too direct an approach toward citizen education can be unproductive since people reacting according to a variation of the selectivity principle feel it necessary to resist that which is either too novel and unfamiliar or too manifestly designed to be manipulative. Even the most docile and tradition-attached population can sense the humor and the wisdom in frustrating those who have authority and are their intellectual betters whenever they become too intent upon changing the ways of others.

Our conclusion may thus be that even though the mass media have great potential for citizenship training in the new states this potential can be realized only through a subtle and understanding approach. For example, new messages and new ideas may be more readily accepted if they are related to old symbols and concepts. Indeed, it generally seems to be the case in most transitional societies that the material which surrounds the explicitly political communications and is in a sense a part of the context of a general learning process is likely to be more significant in influencing attitudes than the directly political material.

CHAPTER IX

Armies in the Process of Political Development

O NLY A few years ago it was generally assumed that the future of the newly emergent states would be determined largely by the activities of their Westernized intellectuals, their socialistically inclined bureaucrats, their nationalist ruling parties, and possibly their menacing communist parties.* It occurred to few students of the underdeveloped regions that the military might become the critical group in shaping the course of nation-building. Now that the military has become the key decision-making element in at least eight of the Afro-Asian countries, we are confronted with the awkward fact that there has been almost no scholarly research on the role of the military in the political development of the new states.

The trend of recent years toward increased authoritarian rule and army-dominated governments raises questions which seem only to emphasize the limitations of our knowledge. Is it true, as we have always supposed, that any encroachment of the military into civilian rule is a blow to liberal government

* This chapter first appeared in John J. Johnson, ed., *The Role of the Military in Developing Countries,* and is reprinted with the kind permission of the Princeton University Press.

and civil liberties? Or is it possible that military rule can in fact establish the necessary basis for the growth of effective representative institutions? Have events reached such a state in parts of Asia that we should welcome army rule as the least odious of possible developments and probably the only effective counterforce to communism? [1] We seem to be confronted by two conflicting images of the politician in uniform. The first, derived largely from Latin America and the Balkans, is that of administrative incompetence, inaction, and authoritarian, if not reactionary, values. The second and more recent is that of a dynamic and self-sacrificing military leadership committed to progress and the task of modernizing transitional societies that have been subverted by the "corrupt practices" of politicians. How is it possible to tell in any particular case whether army rule will lead to sterile authoritarianism or to vigorous development? [2]

These considerations suggest that it might be useful to organize our analysis of the political role of the army, first, with respect to the political implications of the army as a modern institution that has been somewhat artificially introduced into disorganized transitional societies; and second, with respect to the role that such an army can play in shaping attitudes toward modernity in other spheres of society. By such an approach we may hope to locate some of the critical factors for explaining why it is that the military has been a vigorous champion of progress and development in some countries and a retarding influence in others. We may also hope to gain a basis for judging the probable effectiveness of armies in promoting national development and eventually democratic practices.

[1] Guy J. Pauker, "Southeast Asia as a Problem Area in the Next Decade," *World Politics*, XI, No. 3 (April 1959) 325-45.

[2] For an excellent analysis of the military in the developing areas and particularly of the relationship of the army to different types of developing systems see Morris Janowitz, *The Military in the Political Development of New Nations* (Chicago: University of Chicago Press, 1964).

THE ARMY AS A MODERN ORGANIZATION

In large measure the story of the underdeveloped countries is one of countless efforts to create organizations by which resources can be effectively mobilized for achieving new objectives. This is the problem of establishing organizations that, as rationalized structures, are capable of relating means to ends. The history of much of the Western impact on traditional societies fits comfortably within this theme, for the businessman, planter, and miner, the colonial administrator, the missionary, and the educator each in his own way strives to fit modern organizations into tradition-bound societies. Similarly, the story of the nationalists and of the other Westernized leaders can be treated on essentially identical terms, for they, too, try to change the habits of their people by creating modern organizations.

Needless to say, there are not many bright spots in this history, and it is open to question who has been the more tragically heroic or comically futile: the Westerners struggling to establish their organizations in traditional societies, or the nationalist politician and the indigenous adminstrator endeavoring to create a semblance of order out of chaos. On balance, the attempts to establish military organizations seem to have been noticeably the most successful.

It would be wrong to underestimate the patient care that has gone into developing and training colonial armies, and in the newly independent countries the military have been treated relatively generously in the allocation of scarce resources. But in comparison to the efforts that have been expended in developing, say, civil administration and political parties, it still seems that modern armies are somewhat easier to create in transitional societies than are most other forms of modern social structures. The significant fact for our consideration is that the armies created by colonial administration and by the newly emergent countries have been consistently among the most modernized institutions in their societies. Viewed historically, some of these armies have been distinguished: the Indian Army, the Malay Regiments, the Philippine Scouts, the

Arab Legion, the Gurkha Regiments, and the King's Own African Rifles, to mention only the more celebrated ones.

It would take us too far afield to explore the relative advantages military leaders have in seeking to establish armies in transitional societies. We need only note that there is a paradoxical relationship between ritualized and rationalized modes of behavior that may account for the ease with which people still close to a traditional order adapt themselves to military life. Viewed from one perspective, a military establishment comes as close as any human organization can to the ideal type for an industrialized and secularized enterprise. Yet from another point of view the great stress placed on professionalism and the extremely explicit standards for individual behavior make the military appear to be a more sacred than secular institution. If discipline is needed to minimize random and unpredictable behavior, it is also consonant with all the demands that custom and ritual make in the most tradition-bound organization.

For these reasons, and for others related to the hierarchic nature of the organization, the division between traditional and rationally oriented behavior is not very great within armies.[3] Indeed, in any army there is always a struggle going on between tradition and reason. Historically during periods of little change in the state of military technology the tendency has been for the nonrational characteristics to become dominant.[4] Given this inherent conflict in any military organization the question arises concerning why the forces of custom and ritual do not readily dominate the armies of the newly emergent countries and so cause them to oppose the forces of

[3] It is significant that the most common weaknesses of civil bureaucracies in the new countries — like exaggerating the importance of procedure to the point of ritualizing the routine, and the lack of initiative and of a pragmatic and experimental outlook — are not as serious drawbacks of smooth functioning of military establishments. On the contrary, the very qualities that have hobbled civil administration in these countries have given strength and rigidity to their military establishments.

[4] The classic discussion of the spirit of militarism as contrasted with the rational military mind is Alfred Vagts, *A History of Militarism: Romance and Realities of a Profession* (New York: W. W. Norton, 1937).

change. In societies where traditional habits of mind are still strong we might expect the military to be strongly conservative. Such was largely the case in the West during the preindustrial period. By contrast, in most of the newly emergent countries armies have tended to emphasize a rational outlook and to champion responsible change and national development.

This state of affairs is largely explained by the extent to which the armies in these countries have been influenced by contemporary Western military technology. In particular, nearly all of the new countries have taken the World War II type of army as their model.[5] In so doing they have undertaken to create a form of organization that is typical of, and peculiar to, the most highly industrialized civilization yet known. Indeed, modern armies are essentially industrial-type entities. Thus the armies of the new countries are instinct with the spirit of rapid technological development.

The fact that these new armies in preindustrial societies are modeled after industrial-based organizations has many implications for their political roles. One of their characteristics is particularly significant: the specialization that modern armies demand in skills and functions is only distantly related to the command of violence. There has generally been a tremendous increase in the number of officers assigned to staff functions as contrasted with line commands. As the armies have striven to approximate their ideal models they have had to establish all manner of specialized organizations and departments that require skills that are either in short supply or nonexistent in their societies. The Burmese Army, for example, in addition to its engineer and signal corps has special sections on chemical warfare, psychological warfare, and even a historical and archaeological section. All the new armies have attempted to in-

[5] World War II was in itself a decisive event in the birth of many of these countries and, of course, the availability of large quantities of surplus equipment and arms made it realistic to aspire to a modernized army. American military aid has contributed toward making the military the most modernized element not only in recipient countries, but also in neighboring countries which have felt the need to keep up with technological advances.

troduce specialized training schools and advanced techniques of personnel management and procurement. Consequently numbers of the more intelligent and ambitious officers have had to be trained in industrial skills more advanced than those common to the civilian economy.

The high proportion of officers assigned to staff functions means that large numbers of officers are forced to look outside their society for their models. The fact that army leaders, particularly the younger and more ambitious, generally come from those trained in staff positions means that they are extremely sensitive to the needs of modernization and technological advancement. This kind of sensitivity bears little relationship to the command of physical violence and tests of human endurance — in short, to the martial spirit as we customarily think of it. In consequence the officers often find that they are spiritually in tune with the intellectuals, students, and those other elements in society most anxious to become a part of the modern world. They may have little in common with the vast majority of the men they must command. In this respect the gap between the officer class and the troops, once largely a matter of social and economic class (as it still is to some degree), has now been widened by differences in the degree of acculturation to modern life.

It should be noted that these revolutionary changes in military life have significantly influenced the status of the military profession in different societies and hence have had an interesting effect on relative national power. Cultures that looked down on the military at an earlier stage of technology now accord high prestige to the same profession as it has raised its technology. For example, when armies depended entirely on human energy and animal power the Chinese placed the soldier near the bottom of the social hierarchy; with present levels of advanced military technology the soldier is now near the top of the social scale in both Communist and non-Communist China. The change has been more in the nature of the military profession than in basic Chinese cultural values. Conversely, peoples once considered "martial" may now show little interest in, or aptitude for, the new kind of soldiering.

Above all else, however, the revolution in military technology has caused the army leaders of the newly emergent countries to be extremely sensitive to the extent to which their countries are economically and technologically underdeveloped. Called upon to perform roles basic to advanced societies, the more politically conscious officers can hardly avoid being aware of the need for substantial changes in their own societies.

It might seem that those occupying positions in other modern-type organizations in underdeveloped societies would also feel much the same need for change. To whatever extent this may be so, three distinctive features of armies seem to make them somewhat more dynamic in demanding changes.

First of all, armies by nature are rival institutions in the sense that their ultimate function is the test of one against the other. All other organizations operate within the context of their own society; although their initial inspiration may have come from abroad, their primary focus is on internal developments. The civil bureaucracy, for example, can, and indeed has to, deal with its domestic problems with little regard for what other bureaucracies in other countries are doing. The soldier, however, is constantly called upon to look abroad and to compare his organization with foreign ones. He thus has a greater awareness of international standards and a greater sensitivity to weaknesses in his own society.

Second, armies for all their concern with rationality and becoming highly efficient machines are relatively immune to pragmatic tests of efficiency on a day-to-day basis. Armies are created for future contingencies, and in many underdeveloped countries these contingencies have never had to be faced. Even in countries such as Burma and Indonesia, where the army is forced to deal with internal security problems, the effects have been mainly to increase the resources available for building up the army according to the ideal model, with remarkably few concessions being made to practical needs. Other modernized organizations in underdeveloped societies have to cope with more immediate and day-to-day problems; hence they must constantly adjust themselves to local conditions. They cannot adhere as rigidly as armies can to their Western prototypes. Just as Western armies have often existed in a dream world of planning for types of wars that never occur, so armies of underdeveloped countries can devote themselves to becoming modernized and more "efficient" with little regard to immediate reality. Members of other modern-type organizations may desire to see social change in their society, but they are likely to be more conscious of the need to accommodate their ambitions to existing conditions.

Finally, armies always stand at some distance from their civilian societies and are even expected to have ways of their own, including attitudes and judgments, that are remote if not completely apart from those of civilian life. Thus again armies of the newly emergent countries can feel somewhat divorced from the realities of a transitional society and focus more on the standards common to the more industrialized world. In consequence they are often unaware of the difficulties inherent in modernizing other segments of their society. Within their tradition all problems can be overcome if the right orders are given.

ARMIES AS MODERNIZING AGENTS

So much for the army as one of the more modernized of the authoritative agencies of government in transitional societies. When we consider it as a modernizing force for the whole of society, we move into a less clearly defined area where the number of relevant considerations becomes much greater and where we are likely to find greater differences from country to country. Indeed, we shall be able to deal only generally with the social and political aspects of military service and some of the more indirect influences of armies on civilian attitudes.

In all societies it is recognized that armies must make those who enter them into the image of the good soldier. The underdeveloped society adds a new dimension: the good soldier is also to some degree a modernized man. Thus it is that the armies in the newly emergent countries come to play key roles in the process by which traditional ways give way to more Westernized ideas and practices. The very fact that the recruit must break his ties and associations with civilian life and adjust to the more impersonal world of the army tends to emphasize the fundamental nature of this process, which involves the movement out of the particularistic relationships of traditional life and into the more impersonal and universalistic relationships of an industrialized society.

Army training is thus consistent with the direction taken by the basic process of acculturation in traditional societies. Within the army, however, the rate of acculturation is greatly accelerated. This fact contributes to the tendency of army officers to underestimate the difficulties of changing the civilian society.

Probably the most significant feature of the acculturation process as it takes place under the auspices of the army is that it provides a relatively high degree of psychological security. The experience of breaking from the known and relatively sheltered world of tradition and moving into the more unknown modern world is generally an extremely traumatic one. In contrast to the villager who is caught up in the process of being urbanized, the young army recruit from the village has the more sheltered, the more gradual introduction into the modern world. It is hardly necessary to point out the disturbing fact that the urbanization process as it has taken place in most Asian, African, and Latin American societies has generally tended to produce a highly restless, insecure population. Those who have been forced off the land or attracted to the cities often find themselves in a psychologically threatening situation. These are the people who tend to turn to extremist politics and to look for some form of social and personal security in political movements that demand their total commitment. In contrast, those who are exposed to a more technologically advanced way of life in the army find that they must make major adjustments, but that these adjustments are all treated explicitly and openly. In the army one can see what is likely to happen in terms of one's training and one's future. This is not the case in the city.

It should also be noted that the acculturative process in the army often tends to be more thorough and of a broader scope than the urbanization process. In all the main Asian cities there are those who still follow many of the habits and practices of the village. They may live still within the orbit of their family and have only limited outside associations and contacts. These people have made some adjustment to the modern world, but they are likely to be faced with even more in the future, and thus they remain potential sources of political tension.

It should also be noted that the acculturative process in the army tends to be focused on acquiring technical skills that are of particular value for economic development. Just as the army represents an industrialized organization, so must those who have been trained within it learn skills and habits of mind which would be of value in other industrial organizations. In the West, armies have played a very important role in providing technical training and even direct services in the process of industrial development. The German Army trained large numbers of noncommissioned officers who performed important functions as foremen in the German steel mills and in other industries. In the United States the Corps of Engineers played a central role in the whole development of the West; and after the Civil War army veterans provided considerable amounts of the skill and knowledge which, when combined with the influx of immigrants, provided a basis for much of our industrial development. In Latin America the Brazilian Army has played an important part in opening the interior, in promoting the natural sciences, and in protecting the Indian population. In Asia too we can see much the same story being enacted now. Before the war the compulsory training in the Japanese Army provided the whole society with increasing reservoirs of manpower that contributed directly to the development of an industrial society. Army veterans in India have played an important role not only in lower-level industrial jobs but also in managerial positions. In Malaya and the Philippines the army has been the main instrument for training people in operating and maintaining motor vehicles and other forms of machinery.

Politically the most significant feature of the process of acculturation within the army is that it usually provides some form of training in citizenship. Recruits with traditional backgrounds must learn about a new world in which they are identified with a larger political self. They learn that they stand in some definite relationship to a national community. In this sense the army experience tends to be a politicizing experience. Even if recruits are not given explicit training in political matters, they are likely to learn that events in their society are determined by human decisions and not just by chance and fate. Within the army the peasant may come to realize that much in life can be changed and that commands and wishes have consequences. Thus even aside from any formal training in patriotism the recruit is likely to achieve some awareness of the political dimensions of his society. It is therefore not surprising that in many of the newly emergent countries veterans have had appreciable political influence even after only limited military experience.

Armies in the newly emergent countries can thus provide a sense of citizenship and an appreciation of political action. In some cases this can lead to a more responsible nationalism. The recruit may be impressed with the fact that he must make sacrifices to achieve the goals of nationalism and that the process of nation-building involves more than just the shouting of slogans. At the same time there is always the potential danger that the armies will become the center of hypernationalistic movements, as in the case of prewar Japan.

Because the army represents one of the most effective channels for upward social mobility, military-inspired nationalism often encompasses a host of personalized emotions and sentiments about civilian society. Invariably the men, and sometimes even the officers, come from extremely humble circumstances, and it is only within the army that they are first introduced to the possibility of systematically advancing themselves. In transitional societies, where people's station in life is still largely determined by birth and by chance opportunities, powerful reactions usually follow from placing people in a position where they can recognize a definite and predictable relationship between effort and reward. The practice of giving advancement on merit can encourage people, first, to see the army as a just organization deserving of their loyalties, and then possibly to demand that the same form of justice reign throughout their society.

Those who do move up to positions of greater respect and power through the army may often carry with them hostilities toward those with greater advantages and authority in civilian society. The tendency of the military to question whether the civilian elite achieved their station by merit adds another conflict to civil-military relations in most underdeveloped countries. More often than not the military show these feelings by seeking to make national loyalty and personal sacrifice the crucial test of national leadership.

The relationship between armies and civilian leaders varies of course according to the circumstances of historic development. There are first those patterns of development in which the military stand out because in a disrupted society they represent the only effectively organized element capable of competing for political power and formulating public policy. This situation is most likely to exist when the traditional political order, but not necessarily the traditional social order, has been violently disrupted and it becomes necessary to set up representative institutions before any of the other modern-type political organizations have been firmly established. The outstanding example of this pattern of development is modern China from the fall of the Manchu dynasty in 1911 to the victory of the Communists. It is possible to think of this period as one dominated by a constant struggle to escape from the grim circumstances that obtained when only military organizations survived the fall of the traditional systems. Hence the military became the only effective political entity. Thereafter nothing could be done without them, and yet the military could do little without effective civilian institutions. Comparable situations seem to exist at present in some Middle Eastern countries where Western influence brought a commitment to republican institutions but left the army as the only effective modern political structure in the entire society.

A second category includes those countries where the military, while formally espousing the development of democracy, actually monopolizes the political arena and forces any emerging civilian elite to concentrate on economic and social activities. In many ways this arrangement is reminiscent of the Belgian variety of colonialism. At present, the most outstanding example of this form of rule is Thailand.

A third major category, which is probably the largest, consists of those countries in which the organization and structures essential to democratic government exist but have not been able to function effectively. The process of modernization has been retarded to such a point that the army, as the most modernized organization in the society, has assumed an administrative role and taken over control. In these cases there is a sense of failure in the country, and the military are viewed as possible saviors.

It is appropriate to note briefly some of the broader implications of the role of the armies in transitional countries for international stability. The ways in which new societies are being created will have profound significance for the entire world. At the same time it is unrealistic to conclude that the army's role in the new countries is determined only by domestic developments. The nature of the contemporary international order and the focus of Western policies have had a profound influence on military institutions throughout the underdeveloped areas.

There has been a tendency in some quarters to regard the trend toward military rule as favorable to American policy interests. In particular, army rule has been welcomed as promising greater political stability and firmer policies against communism. Unfortunately, in the past we have generally been poor judges of leadership in the new countries. In fact we have been so anxious to wish the new countries well that we have not been very realistic in appraising their national leadership. We have often placed faith in, and indeed lionized, men who are mediocre by any standard of measurement. The fault is more serious than just a misplaced sense of charitableness, for by refusing to employ realistic standards of judgment we encourage the lack of realism and even quackery in the political life of many of these countries.

In seeking a realistic estimate of the potential role of the military in the political development of particular countries it is also necessary to avoid being excessively influenced by ideological considerations that may be relevant only in advanced societies. We have in mind in particular the Western stereotype of the military as a foe of liberal values. This bias, for example, tends at present to take the form of seeing "military aid" as a threat to economic and political development and of assuming that only "economic aid" can make a positive contribution to such form of development. In some cases military aid has in fact made substantial contributions to road building, health facilities, communications networks, and the like, all of which have directly facilitated economic growth. In other cases it has been equally clear that our military aid has seriously retarded economic development by diverting an excessive amount of the nation's energies into unproductive channels. The point is only that in our thinking about the newly emergent countries we must avoid stereotypes and expect many paradoxes.

If we are able to do so, we shall be less surprised to note, for example, that it has been through the military that we have best been able to establish effective relations with the most strongly neutralist nations in Southeast Asia. With both Burma and Indonesia we have had considerable difficulties in almost every dimension of our relationships. We have, however, been able to develop more genuine and straightforward relations with their military than with any other political element. Out of these relations have come further possibilities for cooperation. Thus, rather ironically, after the Burmese terminated our program of economic assistance to them, it was possible to reestablish such assistance only by first providing them with military aid. In this way confidence was reestablished and the stage set for their reacceptance of economic aid.

This particular example may point up a most important consideration about armies in the new countries. For the various reasons which we have mentioned the army is often the most modernized public organization in an underdeveloped country, and as a consequence its leaders often feel more self-confident and are more able to deal frankly and cordially with representatives of industrialized countries. Military leaders are often far less suspicious of the West than civilian leaders because they themselves are more emotionally secure. This sense of security makes it possible for army leaders to look more realistically at their countries. All of these considerations make it easier for the military leaders to accept the fact that their countries are weak and the West is strong without becoming emotionally disturbed or hostile toward the West. Since these leaders seem to have less need to avoid realities, they are in fact easier people with whom to deal and to carry on straightforward relations.

It is important, however, to note from the example that it is possible, and indeed it is essential, to expand a narrow relationship with the military into a much broader one. Military aid has had to become economic aid. Satisfactory relations with the military can become a dead end, just as military rule itself can become sterile, if it does not lead to an interest in total national development.

This is only to say that while it may be possible to find in the armies of underdeveloped countries an element of stability, we should not confuse this with political stability for the entire society. The military may provide an opportunity and a basis for cooperation, but the objective must remain the development of stable representative institutions and practices. In planning for this objective it is essential to conceive of it as involving far more than just the efficient administration of public policies. It is necessary to keep in mind that in the past the West has come to these societies largely in the guise of administrators. This was the nature of colonialism, and we have tended to step into this role with our emphasis upon economic aid. In cooperating with the military we again are essentially strengthening this role of the administrator. In most underdeveloped countries there is at present a genuine need to improve the standards of public administration. In fact, unless such improvements take place they will be able to realize few of their national goals. However, there is a deeper problem, and this is the problem of developing effective relations between the administrators and the politicians. The disturbing fact is that we can with relative ease help people perform administrative roles, but we have not been particularly successful in devising ways of training people to the role of the democratic politician. In many respects this difficulty is the heart of the problem in our relations with the new countries.

This leads us to the conclusion that the military in the underdeveloped countries can make a major contribution to strengthening essentially administrative functions. If the new countries are to become modern nation-states, they will have to have a class of competent administrators. They will also have to have responsible and skilled politicians. In cooperating with the military in these countries we should therefore recognize that they can contribute to only a limited part of national development. In particular, in assisting them to raise standards in the realm of public administration we should also make certain that our assistance does not lead to a stifling of an even more basic aspect of political development: the growth of responsible and representative politicians.

CHAPTER X

The Prospects for Development

A s WE noted at the outset of this study the initial excitement
and enthusiasm which accompanied the ending of the colonial era and the inauguration of independent states has
gradually been dissipated in much of the world as people have
come to learn that political development is not easy. In country after country in Asia and Africa, citizens tend increasingly
to assume that officials are generally corrupt and that the realities of government and politics are far removed from the aspirations of national development.

Prime Minister Nehru after fifteen years of Indian independence told a news conference: "An atmosphere is growing
in India that I find not only disturbing but suffocating." He
found his work was that of "some kind of robot or automa-
ton . . . I was physically fit but getting querulous. I sense
coarseness and vulgarity growing in our public life. In the
Congress Party and the whole country idealism is fading out.
We in India suffer from a split personality. One part is of the
highest moral standard. The other part completely forgets
about it. We are losing our sense of mission. What to do? I
don't know." [1]

There is danger that in the West a similar mood of disillu-
sion, if not cynicism, will replace the earlier spirit of sympathy

[1] Quoted in I. R. Sinai, *The Challenge of Modernisation* (London:
Chatto & Windus, 1964) p. 75.

for people presumably inspired by a revolution of rising expectations. After a decade of foreign-aid programs and billions of dollars of our assistance, people are beginning to wonder in increasing numbers what it will all lead to. In America a form of neo-isolationism has arisen as spokesmen argue that we must try to do less abroad and more at home with our own islands of poverty. But the outside world keeps pressing in on us, and it demands our attention. The need is for realism in our search for understanding about the processes of political change.

In seeking to make realistic forecasts about the developing areas we must first note that the discovery of science and rationality that man can and should control both his future and his environment can produce faith in new forms of magic. Once it seems possible to grasp a problem intellectually and to solve it technically, then it may seem as though there is no reason why wishes should not become realities. One result of this kind of thinking is the assumption by technocrats that the only impediment to intellectually conceivable development must be the perverseness and irrationality of lesser men. This may appear to be confirmed by the fact that other peoples have developed amazing economies and powerful polities, which suggests what has been done in one place can be done throughout the world. Where development does not take place, this can seem to mean there are disturbing differences in the capacities of different cultures, if not of different peoples. Thus the discovery of science and rationality and the mere extension of knowledge to other societies can bring with it anxieties about a people's own society. To suppress these anxieties it may be necessary for them to try to believe that everything is possible and that everything must be made possible in the shortest order of time.

Against these views of the feasibility of development stand the issues of effort and time. The process of translating idealized plans into realities always calls for far more effort than rationality usually suggests. And a contemporary look at life in the industrially advanced societies does not always readily communicate the fact that tremendous feats of effort were necessary to create them and are still necessary to maintain their economic and political forms.[2] Time, too, is essential, not only to establish the necessary habits of mind and institutionalization of practices but to reap the cumulative effects of compound interest, for most forms of economic and social advance depend upon gradual accumulations of capital — these can be painfully slow when starting from humble bases. Thus in countries which are making what must be recognized as technically impressive progress of, say, over 5 percent-a-year growth in per capita production, the visible effects may be very little, and people can become discouraged and impatient. Optimum growth rates can seem depressingly trivial for people who once wanted to believe in magic.

Precisely because nationalism seems to be such an automatic, unreflecting, and spontaneous matter requiring neither careful planning nor sophisticated acts, it is hard for people to appreciate that a functioning modern nation is one of the most complex and intricate products of human culture. It is the most elaborate and extensive form of human organization man has yet evolved. Political development must thus be seen as an extraordinarily costly enterprise in terms of the investment of effort and resources. It is an enterprise calling for patience and human understanding.[3]

THE PROSPECTS FOR STABILITY

Much of the discouragement of the last few years stems from the number of cases in which attempts at democracy have failed and armies and soldiers or autocrats and demagogs have taken over in the name of stability and anti-corruption. This

[2] One of the features of David McClelland's work on achievement motivation is to suggest there is a very close relationship between effort and development and people in the more developed societies do work harder than people with less opportunities. See David C. McClelland, "National Character and Economic Growth in Turkey and Iran," in Lucian W. Pye, ed., *Communications and Political Development* (Princeton: Princeton University Press, 1963).

[3] For an excellent discussion of the effort called for to insure economic development but not in a defeatist spirit see Robert Heilbrouner, *The Great Ascent* (New York: Harper & Row, 1963); and William McCord, *The Springtime of Freedom* (New York: Oxford University Press, 1965).

unhappy trend has stemmed in part from a much too cavalier attitude about the possibilities of democracy among unsophisticated peoples.

It also reflects the fact that the strata of Westernized leaders who assumed power immediately upon independence did not have deep roots in their societies. The cosmopolitan elements in such countries as Burma, Indonesia, Cambodia, and even India have had to yield ground to more parochial segments of their societies. Provincial and state leaders have challenged the authority of the Westernized and socialist-liberal generation of leaders who inspired the drives toward independence.

As the less cosmopolitan and the more parochial elements have acquired power the political processes of the new states have moved away from the standards of the Western world toward more indigenous ones. The result has been often a decline in efficiency and in standards of justice, but a rise in stability. Governments have sought less to change their citizens and more to accommodate themselves to existing conditions. The Congress Party in India, which once was inspired by reformist sentiments, has become increasingly an institution adjusting to local community power realities in each constituency.[4]

The groping search for stability is motivated in most new states by a realization of the uncertainty of their authority on the part of rulers who have learned they cannot command as much as they would like. When government was only a question of filling the vacated posts of withdrawing colonial officials and of proclaiming the desirability of idealistic conditions, few people were sensitive to the limits of authority in chaotically organized societies. Governments boldly took the lead in assuming they could solve all problems, whether those of planning change at every level or adjudicating conflicts

---

4 For a very illuminating and sophisticated argument that the decline in the cosmopolitan component of the Indian political culture and the rise in the more parochial will advance modernization in India see Myron Weiner, "India: Two Political Cultures," in Lucian W. Pye and Sidney Verba, eds., *Political Culture and Political Development* (Princeton: Princeton University Press, 1965).

among all interests. Gradually, however, leaders have experienced the shock of realizing the limits of their power and of discovering that authority dissolves when it attempts more than it can achieve.[5]

In an absolute sense there has not been enough power in the new states to meet all the demands on governments. Once rulers sense their own inadequacies, others soon sense them. The rules of law and custom that seemed relatively firm at one time are challenged or ignored with increasing impunity.[6]

The result has been a profound crisis of authority in country after country. The unquestioned authority of national leaders and of nationalist movements has given way to more limited powers. Failure to realize promised goals brought in its wake doubts about the legitimacy of once pretentious power. At present in most transitional societies, new and inherently limited forms of power are seeking the necessary degree of acceptance in order to become new forms of authority.

The test for authority is in part a moral matter and in part a matter of competence. The uncertain pattern of change, however, has left great confusion about what should be the general basis for morality; and the ever-increasing problems of public policy have made it distressingly difficult to prove competence. Only if advancement can be seen in more incremental terms will it be possible for temporary power holders to prove their competence. Thus, in several new states there have been significant advances in development in spite of the absence of dramatic efforts, for in these settings leaders have been quietly proving their competence against realistic standards of performance.

THE UNEVEN PATTERN OF DEVELOPMENT

In speaking of the trend from idealism to cynicism and of the crises of authority we have been dealing with a relatively

[5] For a discussion on the limits of authority in contemporary India and Burma see I. R. Sinai, *op. cit.*

[6] On the concept of absolute levels of power as related to political development see Frederick W. Frey, "Political Development, Power, and Communications in Turkey," in Pye, ed., *op. cit.*

universal pattern of the last decade. During these years it has been possible to treat on a collective basis most of the problems of development in the new states, for the processes have been remarkably widespread. More recently, however, differences have become more conspicuous. Some countries have been slower than others in entering their times of crises; more importantly, some seem to be surmounting their problems of authority far more effectively than others.

As a consequence, it appears certain that in the years ahead differences in the experiences of the new states will be increasing, and generalizing about conditions in the underdeveloped areas will become more difficult. We are moving toward a world that will be composed of numerous categories of developing countries. Some like Malaysia, the Philippines, and Pakistan are likely to show impressive yearly advances in economic growth, maintain relative stability in their patterns of rule, and foster rising standards of justice. Others such as India may not be able to make as impressive economic advances, but they may be equally impressive in coping with the problems of transferring power. Still other states, such as Nigeria, may have certain key problems, like ethnic and regional integration, which if surmounted will open the way to significant advances in all other fields.

On the other hand, there are countries in which progress will certainly be painfully slow and the very infrastructure essential for further development may take a generation or more to build. In some such countries the impeding force exists in current generation of leaders, and little can be expected until they are replaced. In all too many countries the power holders for personal reasons, either ideological or material, find it profitable to block all possibilities for broader national development.

The inevitable consequence is increasingly different patterns of development among the new states. No longer are all the developing countries confronting the same problems, and increasingly they tend to have quite different interests. This will surely result in a rising level of tension among the new states and a decline in the possibilities of Afro-Asian unity.

In the first years after independence most new states are absorbed with their domestic problems and their relations with the industrial powers which are the sources of economic assistance and technical skills. Gradually, however, neighbors come to know neighbors; and the consequence is new tensions in the world. Thus the dreams of pan-Africanism have turned into the complex politics of incipient blocs confronting each other in a struggle to insure national security in a tumultuous continent. In Southeast Asia every country has some border conflict with a neighbor.

Countries making substantial progress in building national unity and achieving economic growth tend often to become the objects of envy and jealousy felt by states facing failure. This kind of situation is one reason for Sukarno's policy of Indonesian confrontation of Malaysia. Shifting prospects of development have contributed to repeated renewals of tension between India and Pakistan; in north Africa, relations among Egypt, Algeria, and Morocco are certain to be influenced greatly by their relative degrees of success in development.

The change from a condition in which most underdeveloped countries felt they were in the same boat to one in which some are clearly better off than others is bound to alter the nature of Afro-Asian interstate relations. What brought together the Afro-Asian nations in the first instance was the feeling they shared a common grievance over their colonial experience and, in facing the problems of development, they had a common set of interests. During this period, leadership in the Afro-Asian world really meant being a model underdeveloped country capable of commanding the attention of the great powers and prodding them to provide greater assistance to the underdeveloped areas. Thus during the 1950's when India, under Nehru, sought to be the leader of the "third world," he followed a strategy of focusing not on India's relations with the other underdeveloped countries but upon her relations with Washington, Moscow, and London.

In more recent years as the differences among the developing nations have become more conspicuous the Afro-Asian world has produced its own intense internal politics. Leadership in the Afro-Asian world involves the capacity to influence other Afro-Asian governments without regard to relations with the great powers. For example, in the mid-1960's when Communist China began to seek leadership of the Afro-Asian states she concentrated on applying pressures to select African and Asian governments and acted as though the rest of the world might be ignored as far as Afro-Asian politics were concerned. This was exactly opposite to the earlier approach of India. The Indian style was similar to that used by a schoolboy seeking to be the leader of his class by the way he handles his relations with his teacher, at times by trying to embarrass the teacher but ultimately by seeking to win the teacher's approval. The Chinese approach is that of the schoolboy who seeks leadership not via the classroom but on the playground where teachers are not present.

In all likelihood politics among the developing areas is going to become increasingly intense. Different states at different degrees of development are going to see the world in different terms. Some of the countries presently feel they are on the road of progress and need stability, and thus they tend to react against the more radical proposals of those countries with little hope for progress. Also many of the developing nations have come to realize it is a competitive world when it comes to obtaining foreign aid, and the rich countries are tending to be increasingly discriminating in providing aid.[7] Thus the developing countries are appreciating more and more the importance of influencing the criteria used in allocating aid. Different criteria produce different distributions of aid, so the countries must inevitably compete against each other.

THE NORTH-SOUTH PROBLEM

If we foresee correctly that there are going to be increasing differences in interests among the developing countries, then it seems unlikely a sharp clash between the industrial countries and the united masses of the developing countries will emerge.

[7] John D. Montgomery, *The Politics of Foreign Aid* (New York: Praeger, 1962); Edward Mason, *Economic Planning in Underdeveloped Areas* (New York: Fordham University Press, 1958).

Some voices have been raised in fear that in the near future world politics will be shaped largely by the clash between the rich nations of the Northern Hemisphere and the poor ones of the Southern.[8] Among Indian spokesmen it has been popular to paraphrase Lincoln and say, "A world that is half rich and half poor cannot long endure." It is true the continued close existence of great extremes in welfare can become intolerable.

Yet, significantly, during the last decade when there was great public attention directed to the problems of development and considerable sentimental, if not ideological, concern about the need to improve conditions in the new states such a cleavage in world politics did not become manifest. This was true in spite of the fact that during the decade the gap in standards of living in the two parts of the world became greater, and not less as everyone had hoped. The confrontation of the future is not likely to be between the industrial countries and the still underdeveloped ones. This is particularly true if there are rising doubts about how rapidly it is possible to bring about all forms of development.

This forecast, however, should not be the cause for comfort. The continued existence of weakness and poverty in much of the world is likely to produce other forms of tension that may possibly constitute a more serious threat to world stability than a direct clash between the rich and the poor states would. The shrinking of the world in terms of communications means tensions and conflicts are likely to be magnified far more effectively than the diffusion of constructive skills and attitudes.

The fact that the world is not likely to be sharply divided according to a direct north-south conflict does not mean that relations between the industrial societies and the developing ones will not be extremely complicated. As we have already observed, the classical Western nation-state system was premised upon a relatively homogeneous cultural base and a common acceptance of certain quasi-legalistic assumptions about the proper forms of interstate relationships. The principles of

[8] See, for example, Gunnar Myrdal, *Rich Lands and Poor* (New York: Harper & Row, 1957); Barbara Ward, *The Rich Nations and the Poor Nations* (London: Hamish Hamilton, 1962).

sovereignty and of non-intervention in the domestic affairs of other states assumed states could readily maintain internal order and provide minimum defenses for the integrity of their societies. These conditions do not exist in the present fragile international system that must encompass both the dynamic industrial societies and the still inchoate nations.

Thus gross uncertainty still prevails about what the basis of relations between the powerful and the weak should be. What once were honorable terms of association now may seem suspect. For example, in the traditional system treaties between sovereigns were both honorable and plausibly reciprocal, while at present, when there is such a gap in power, treaties of alliance can be seen as threats to the integrity if not the sovereignty of the weak. It is impossible to ignore the power considerations; politics involves power, and international politics can be no different from domestic politics on this score.

For several reasons during the decades since World War II the realities of power have been blurred in the international system, and so the world has not been moving ahead in a purposeful fashion toward a new, realistic international system. The frightening vision of the thermonuclear power capabilities of the United States and Russia has had the effect that neither of the superpowers has been prepared to assert much of its non-nuclear power in its dealings with the rest of the world. At the same time the European powers in withdrawing from their colonial roles have created the illusion that they are less powerful than in fact they are. The combined result of both these tendencies to mask the realities of relative power in the world has been to create the even greater illusion about the potential power of the new states. These considerations combined with the nature of United Nations' politics have understandably made many of the new governments feel they have an influence on world affairs disproportionate to their power. Illusion has compounded delusions.

In the future it would seem the reduction in United States-Soviet tensions and the broadening Sino-Soviet split are likely to produce a world in which relative power is likely to be more sensitively reflected in interstate relations. This trend is likely to be accompanied by a decline in conscious stress upon ideology. When power considerations predominate over ideological ones, politics tends to become less compulsive, more responsible, more pragmatic, and risk-taking assumes a different character.

In many areas we can observe this trend taking shape. There is the changing attitude toward the United Nations and voting in the General Assembly. There is the fact that both the United States and the Soviet Union have become more discriminating and more differentiating in allocating foreign aid. There is evidence that the more successfully developing countries are becoming less ideologically oriented and more impatient with irresponsible international behavior.

The trend, however, is slow. The cold war continues. Little powers still like to indulge their emotions and feel there is profit in insulting the great powers. Rulers who want more resources persist in blackmailing the Americans and Russians who are competing for their good will by threatening to give advantages to the side providing the resources. Irresponsible behavior abounds, and governments as well as people still feel that ideological sloganeering should be given precedence over sober planning for national development.

In short, progress toward a more realistic and responsible form of world politics involving the new states is going to be slow and uncertain. Yet the direction of development is unmistakable, for in all forms of politics stability and justice can be realized only when power and responsibility are recognized and are congruent.

**THE POSITIVE CONTRIBUTIONS OF THE NEW STATES
TO THE WORLD CULTURE**

From an economic perspective it does seem clear that under existing technological conditions the gap between the industrial countries and the less developed ones is certain to increase. Indeed, within the context of foreseeable human history, equality in living standards among nations will never come about. But this is not a shocking statement, for even in the most affluent countries there will remain great differences from region to region. In fact, the very pattern of technological advance appears to encourage even more differentiated patterns of development.

What counts is the fact that progress is possible everywhere, and that people's satisfaction in life depends upon what is happening immediately about them and not in the technical comparisons of statisticians and economists. Thus the downward spiral of the "revolution of rising frustrations" can be checked with realism and not by trying to arouse again a "revolution of rising expectations."

True, even in the most favorable conditions it is going to take great effort to overcome the weight of prolonged poverty and political impatience. The population explosion, for example, is a very real thing and not just a trick of the mathematicians. In country after country what might have been a dramatic increase in investment and production has in fact meant only that a society is barely able to keep up with its growing numbers. Therefore there is no justification in suggesting that the prospects for economic development in much of the world are anything but dim.

Yet change is taking place. Dimensions of the world culture are spreading, and more and more people throughout the world are sharing common experiences. Before long almost all mankind will encounter in childhood the disciplining effects of the classroom and know what it means to read printed symbols and to accept the unchallengeable facts of mathematics. After the common experiences of education there will be the universal problems of jobs, money, and personal advancement.

Once these minimum standards are achieved and as countries increasingly resolve their basic problems of national identity and find pride in their evolving cultures, then the relations of all parochial cultures to the world culture will take on a new form. No longer will it be possible to confuse the world culture with the particular cultures of Western societies. Instead it will be possible to appreciate the diversities of mankind under terms in which it is possible to recognize the reality of man's equality. Under these conditions people everywhere according to their individual talents can in actuality contribute to the enrichment of the world culture and thus of all human life.

This is what the culture of science has already done in a limited field of human endeavor. The broader world culture will make possible an accumulative sense of advancement, as exists in science, in which all people can participate. Then the statement will be true that everyone can learn from the different ways which others have used to cope with the universal and pedestrian problems of human existence.

Index

201